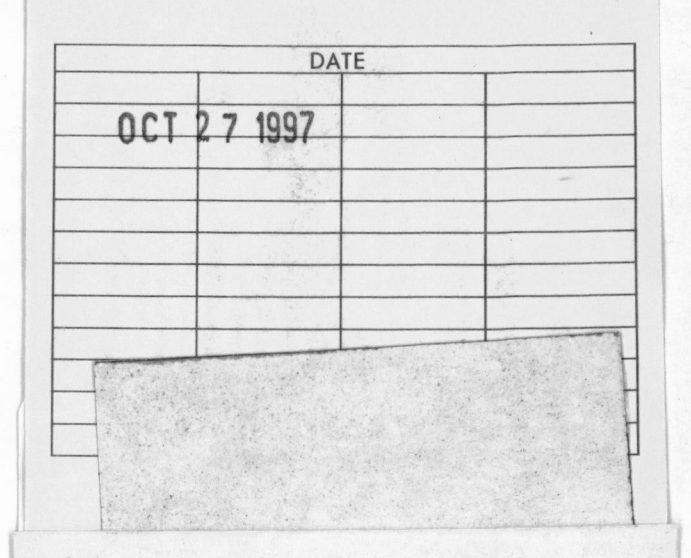

DATE			
OCT 2 7 1997			

ERROL FLYNN
A Memoir

BOOKS BY EARL CONRAD

ERROL FLYNN
A Memoir

BY EARL CONRAD
Illustrated with photographs

DODD, MEAD & COMPANY · NEW YORK

Library of Congress Cataloging in Publication Data

Conrad, Earl.
  Errol Flynn: a memoir.

  1. Flynn, Errol Leslie, 1909–1959. 2. Moving-
picture actors and actresses—United States—
Biography.
PN2287.F55C6   791.43'028'0924 [B]   77–21870
ISBN 0-396-07502-9

FOR ALYSE
My usual dedication to my unusual wife

CONTENTS

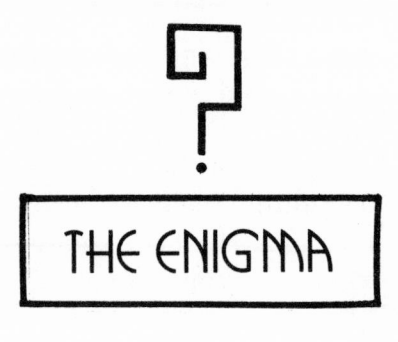

THE ENIGMA

Flat No. 1
4 Rochester Gardens
Hove 3
Sussex
England
Nov. 29, 1961

Dear Mr. Conrad,
I am very grateful indeed for the nice letter you have written
to us recently concerning the last days of Errol and his attitude
towards us, his parents. I do wish we could get together some
time so that perhaps with your help we might be able to solve the
enigma of Errol. . . .

Once more thanks
and sincere regards
from
Theo. T. Flynn

Fifteen years have passed since I received that letter from
the late Professor Theodore T. Flynn, father of Errol Flynn
and husband of the late Marelle Flynn.

For all that time I have been thoughtful about Professor
Flynn's very point—the enigma of the most unforgettable
figure I ever met, after a lifetime of meeting a gamut of

9

those one can meet as a writer, as an occasional book-length biographer and as a literary explorer adventuring through one's time.

No one else I ever met contained the essence of enigma in human form as did the celebrated actor-cavorter.

Flynn, who wore a squarely-shaped question mark on the handkerchief pocket of his suitcoat for half a lifetime, was as much a puzzle to himself as to those who tried to understand him. He wore that question mark because he was nailed by the uncertainty of existence—somewhat crucified by it, as it were—desiring above all things to know the living unknown.

Finally, of course, I knew him better than most of the others I have written about. I return to Errol Flynn because of a deep-seated urge to convey some understanding of the complexities that made him tick.

I knew when I worked with him and from the story that was unfolding—his unknown origins in Tasmania, New Guinea and Australia; his war with his mother; the special influence exerted upon him by his scientist father; his abnormal affinity with water (a closeness more appropriate to a fish than a human being); other strangenesses pertaining to fear of madness and castration—I knew that what appeared at the surface, the publicly cavorting Flynn, was merely the tip of the iceberg. The challenge was to learn the other seven eighths, to discover what "set him off." Even when I finished working on his autobiography, *My Wicked, Wicked Ways,* I privately knew that I only partially understood him.

The tip of the Flynn iceberg has been his image as a lecherous fellow, an actor of considerable attainment, yet primarily the roustabout and ladykiller. But beneath that peak there were many other Flynns: the philosophically curious man, the frustrated writer, the congenital seeker after monogamy who could live only promiscuously, a misdirected scientist whose "experiments" all turned out to be pranks, a wanderer over seas and lands whose travels very probably far exceeded those of the mythical Ulysses, a seeker after elemental meanings that have eluded the whole of mankind as well as himself, a man tormented by his acquisition of the wrong image, a figure of human contradiction whose thoughts and acts were caricatures of caricature itself.

The first half of the twentieth century was lived by him perhaps as wholly and completely as by anyone. We can see in his travels, physical and abstract, the convolutions of history across and around the globe: its wars and revolts and changing moralities, its diversity on all continents. He lived through Stone Age New Guinea on its own prehistoric terms, through colonial Australia into the spiraling technologically modern West, and much else.

A new young generation, which knows that there is such a thing as "the media child," can understand how the newspapers of the world rocked with the daily antics, troubles and affairs of the late Errol for one whole generation. There was no respite in the daily columns, features, articles and radio gossip from the amusing life of the roistering Errol Flynn who graced the screen, sailed the oceans and hid out in enclaves in one place or another, always with some new flame.

I think of Errol as an individual "larger than life," larger than most individuals anyway. He had special parents, a special set of environments and was exposed to unusual cultures, all contributing to create a choice representative of the human species. It was because I perceived him as a kind of special or select figure that the memory of him stayed with me.

The remarkability of him was his individuality, his uniqueness, a certain independence and even wildness, as if he were an untamed brother of the sky, like the wild geese that fly overhead while domesticated geese in their barnyard warrens are limited to looking upward yearningly at the free-flying geese overhead, going hundreds of miles a day north or south.

Errol Flynn was such an untamed brother, and the interest in him is in that image: that's the distillation, the alembic of the man.

This recollection-study-regalement recounts in some large part the last days of Errol Flynn. But in a larger sense it is a search backward into the nodal points of his career for a presentation of clues that may help us to comprehend him.

Having said that, and having ventured into the maze of him, the enigma of him, I can't say that I've solved the riddle—and I'm not sure anyone ever can. But I return to the theme of Errol Flynn because I think it is a big one. Else I do not see why for all these years I have been magnetized by the search for a solution to the enigma his father felt he contained, which I knew was there, and which was intuited by many who were involved in the externals and internals of his life and world.

E. CONRAD

JAMAICA

The smoke of battle was all about me. I was with Pickett at his final charge at Gettysburg. Men were dying all around. I might die. Ninety thousand of Lee's men had been at Chambersburg shortly before, and now they and thousands of others were massed opposite the Union troops. Scores of thousands lay over the battlefield—forever. The noise was overpowering. Shell explosions raged in my ears and I couldn't breathe.

The smoke from my own cigarettes—I had inhaled five or six full cigarettes in the last twenty minutes—mingled with the smoke of the scene as Pickett yelled, "Charge!" I was writing the life story of William Henry and Fanny Seward and the death and destruction all about me in my kitchen where I worked was horrible. Would the Union win or wouldn't it?

The phone rang.

I staggered from my typewriter, breathless, asphyxiated by the Gettysburg smoke and a half pack of Camels.

"Hello."

"Oh hello, Howard." My mind was on Pickett.

"How would you like to go to Jamaica with Errol Flynn?"

"Come again, Howard?"

"How would you like to go to Jamaica with Errol Flynn?"

"What's the deal?"

I stood at the door to Errol's suite on the ninth floor of the Park Lane Hotel for about five minutes. I had knocked three times. He knew I was coming to see him. This was the morning after the call. It was now ten o'clock. I was on time. Where the hell was he?

I heard someone inside futtering with the knob.

A strange being who then didn't seem much taller than I opened the door. He wore a bedraggled robe and was in sandals. I had expected a tall imposing figure to greet me. It seemed his eyes were just a bit above the level of my own. His face looked yellowish, haggard, bloated. That heart color, I thought. Migod. This was the great hero of screen and the public stage? He saw me take him in at a glance, read my discovery, shock and unbelief.

"Come in." The interior was dim, unlighted. "Take a seat. I'll be out in a minute."

I waited.

I waited more. Eight or nine minutes passed.

There was a bedroom door I had my eyes on. He would come out of there and enter the main room, probably dressed and looking better.

Suddenly a pair of panties came flying out that door. The silky thing lofted as if thrown by an expert forward passer, then settled like a butterfly on the floor in the center of the room.

Ho Jesus, what am I into?

A minute later a pixie of a girl came flying out, just like that earlier butterfly. She was half-clad, breastless and breathless, and she said, "He'll be out soon. He's taking a leak."

Pickett . . . Pickett . . . went through my mind.

The girl said, "If all goes well and the deal they've set up with you is okay, we'll be flying out to Jamaica tomorrow."

She vanished back into the bedroom. I could hear the sound of Errol's stream tinkling from the bathroom.

My wife, who is much smarter about many things than I am, said one thing to me before I went downtown to talk over the deal. "Now listen to me. These guys like Flynn are used to pushing people around. Don't let him get you into running his errands. Take a strong stand right away, or you'll be wiping his behind like others have certainly done."

I listened to her.

Because I had listened hard to her for twenty-five years I had been able to publish books regularly.

Flynn came out. He looked taller. His shoulders were squared. He still looked debauched, but taller debauched. He wore a suit, the same suit I saw him wear for the next ten weeks (never another).

"Where's my tie, Dhondi?"

Dhondi? Was that the young lady's name?

"She's my secretary," he said.

Traveling through customs and about the world—she was only fifteen then—some subterfuge was necessary.

He had tried to write his own autobiography, he said, but it was too difficult for him to manage. His publishers had gotten restive and wouldn't let him get out of the contract. I could work with some manuscript he had written in Mex-ico.

"Will you be telling about your trip to Spain with the Loyalists?"

The conversation livened. I had touched a central chord within him. Deep down he imagined himself some kind of a rebel or revolutionist, some kind of politician, some kind of statesman, a man with social awareness and conviction. I had a suspicion of it, and in one fell thrust I hit the mark.

"Sure, sure! You know about that?"

"I've read about your every move. Seen most of your films. I guess everybody has. Been following your fortunes since *Robin Hood* and *Captain Blood* and the 1943 case."

His eyes squinted. They weren't pretty eyes. They never were and he knew they weren't. They were his least feature: small eyes set far apart. Nobody could figure anything from reading this man's eyes. You can periscope your way into some people via their eyes, but not Flynn. His eyes reminded me of William S. Hart's, the old cowboy actor of early cinema history who squinted all the time, reflecting every emotion with a squint: laughter, tragedy, life, death. Flynn had a squint from time to time, that kind of squint.

I had shown that I knew much about him, was interested in him. I mentioned one or two of his wartime pictures: good acting. I knew where and how to touch his artistic concern.

The deal was cementing.

"DRINK!"

It was question and command. The word rang in the room like music. It was the voice of an experienced orator or a statesman saying, "WAR!" It was the voice I had heard from the screen and it was here in person, so it was something more. It was a voice that could resound. It was Britannia rules the waves. *"Drink!"* The echo spattered against the walls of the dim Park Lane room and reverberated.

"Ah uh, not right now." I was sniffing. I had been sniffing ever since I entered the room. There had been a cigarette or something like a cigarette dying in an ashtray. I knew the Deep South and this smelled like magnolia. Very much like magnolia: a sweet, sickening smell.

He and Dhondi watched me sniff and look at the table.

"Are you a square?" he asked. He wondered how much they would be able to get away with if I hung around them.

"Hell no," I said. "God knows, no! God forbid!" But let me tell you something: you do not get to write books if you spend your life on liquor, marijuana and opium. I knew all about alcohol but little or nothing about the others.

There were other details Flynn mentioned, such as my name would not be on the book, and what rights I would have and not have in the finished job. "My lawyer'll be here in a few minutes. He'll have a letter with him. If you sign it we'll get out of here by tomorrow. How do you like to travel, first class or coach?"

"First class," I said, as if anything else was out of the question, as if I always traveled first class. I rarely did.

"I always travel coach," he said.

Actually it dawned on me later that his traveling coach had something to do with a fundamental trait within him, the trait that often got him into trouble. He was a congenital democrat—when he wasn't a confounded imperialist. He had to be with down-and-outers, with the mob, with the plain people—till he was on top of them ten seconds later.

But this time we went first class.

The lawyer arrived. I signed.

I ran over to a ticket office, my first errand for him, to get passage arranged. I bit into my tongue for I had passed up an opportunity at the first instant to reject being a flunky or errand boy. What would my wife say? But he nabbed me for that errand right after I signed, and what else could I do? I would learn he loved to have servants, slaves, aides, flunkies about him. He was a king without a country. Wafts of this aura came to me already, and I knew I was in for something.

One of the fantasies of young women (older ones, too) all over the country at that time was the dream of spending time on a small island somewhere in the world alone with Errol Flynn. A great romantic, a handsome lover, lots of bananas and avocados to pluck right from the trees between love sessions. No dishes to do. An old dream, maybe universal. Maybe females in all ages have had these dreams about the romantic heroes of their own era.

Anyway, by proxy, bygod and by contract, I was on my way to an island in the Caribbean with the great swashbuckler, with of course his small companion, Dhondi, fifteen, lovely to look at: a ginger-tongued butterfly.

At the airport I had the novel experience of observing Flynn get Very Important Person treatment. And as I was part of his retinue of two, something of that significance brushed off on me.

As soon as we walked into the airport, someone waiting for him hastened toward us and said, "This way, Mr. Flynn."

We were shown to the administration office, a three- or

four-minute walk through the port, and we entered a good-sized room that looked official, circumspect. "Take seats. Mr. Blake will be here soon."

Blake, the airport manager, had among other duties meeting celebrities each day and spending a few minutes with them while their passports and clearance were being handled, so that they would not have to put up with the humiliation of standing in line.

We sat waiting. In a little while the airport manager entered. He advanced on Flynn, introduced himself. Then he saw me. He assumed I was an aide, the man to handle Flynn's technical matters. He moved toward me with some papers, saying, "These need to be signed."

This was my chance. I wasn't going to play that role anymore. I was a writer and he needed me, and I meant to stand my ground, as my wife said I must, "Or else you'll be treated as a doormat."

No doormat me, I thought.

I looked at the advancing man steadily, coldly. "I don't usually handle Flynn's private affairs." He stopped in his tracks. Flynn started in his seat, sat upright. Dhondi's mouth fell open and her gum fell out.

The clash of silence lasted about four seconds.

The manager turned edgily toward Flynn and handed him the papers. The crisis was over—I thought.

Actually, what went on in Flynn's mind was this: I won't be able to work with this guy; it'll fall through. He thought I was going to be steadily recalcitrant, cantankerous, impossible to associate with.

This would clear up in time. Three weeks later he told me about the size of that airport crisis, one I never suspected.

We were taken by a jitney on three wheels to the side of the Pan American plane we would be boarding. We hung about awhile, then got the report we would have to go to the airport hotel because the plane needed repair work. Errol knelt down by a wheel and picked up a piece of broken metal. He looked at it in distrust—he was an old hand with planes. "Metal fatigue!" he exclaimed in disgust. "We'll mail this to the company headquarters and tell them to junk this plane." Dhondi took the piece of metal and put it in her pocketbook. I volunteered to write the letter. Somehow that detail, which involved all of us, had nothing to do with following Flynn's whimsies in the fashion required of an orderly.

In the hotel room where we stayed for more than ten hours I had an opening experience that was a shocker.

He asked me how we would be proceeding, how would I take the story.

"When we get there," I explained, "we have to hire a stenographer who can write as fast as you can talk. He takes down the stuff, types it up, turns it over to me as rapidly as he can. We do that until the story is done, until I've pumped you dry, gotten you to look back a lifetime."

"I can arrange that when we get to the Titchfield," he said.

Meantime, I suggested, he could talk freely and I would take raw notes in longhand.

He sipped on vodka from time to time. I began to listen keenly as he seemed to be talking about someone very specifically. He was talking aloud but not exactly to me. He paced about the large room.

"The cunt gave me so much trouble when I was a kid."

I didn't know what he was talking about, whether he was talking about sex or something else.

"She made my life miserable. I hated the cunt."

I made no notes. What the hell was he talking about?

"I ran away from her whenever I could. And while the old man was taking eighty-million-year-old fish out of the ocean she was running around with big shots in Paris—the cunt."

"Who are you talking about?"

Dhondi was off to the side, hiding deep in an upholstered chair, saying nothing, watching each of us in a catlike way.

"My mother. I'm talking about my mother."

"What! Your mother! How can you talk about your mother like that? How can you use that word about your own mother?"

My shock was total. He knew it would be.

He repeated with even more emphasis, *"The cunt."*

Migod, I had never heard any man ever call his mother *that.* And this was just about the first word out of his mouth as soon as we were together in a spot where he could begin talking about himself. What the devil!

Figuring that I had to identify with the man and try to see things the way he saw them, I talked about his mother but referred to her in the same way. "What did the cunt do then?" "How did the cunt behave in that situation?"

It was okay with him. I was in with Flynn. It seemed he rather enjoyed hearing an outsider call his mother by that unmotherly identification.

We set out for Jamaica late at night, and the ride was turbulent. The ship lurched and dropped a few hundred feet. "It's the beginning of the hurricane season in the Carib," he said. "Maybe way up here we've hit some bad winds."

I had eaten improperly before boarding and he commiserated. We gripped the seat belts.

This was the same ship that Errol said had metal fatigue. He was sitting beside me, sober and worried. Dhondi sat opposite.

He ventured a thought, prophetic as it turned out. "What the hell, you or I might be dead a year from now."

We reached Jamaica at four o'clock the next morning. Word of Flynn's arrival at this hour had gotten out in Kingston. A group of young women were waiting patiently at the terminal for his autograph.

Dhondi and I got into a car and waited for him to complete his routine with his admirers. They were black girls, pretty, mostly in their teens.

Someone drove us across the island of Jamaica. It was dark. I knew there was jungle out there—the moon displayed it—but I couldn't make out much. I half slept through the two-hour ride: turning, turning on winding roads, over hills and valleys.

Pickett . . . Pickett . . . something inside me said.

To hell with Pickett . . . I'm into this thing with Errol Flynn.

"I used to own this hotel," Errol said on the day we started to work. He was referring to the Titchfield Hotel where we were staying.

"What made you buy it?"

"I liked the bar."

"What?"

"What I said. I liked the bar."

He went on, "When I first saw the bar and the view of the ocean and Navy Island from here, and the people about the bar were friendly and laughing and inclined to sing, and when they started serving up the drink of the land [that's what he called rum], I decided it was what I needed. I needed a hotel where I could slide down a banister from my quarters upstairs and land at a bar."

Later, in his diary, he expressed some regrets about that inspired moment: "What unfriendly planetary influences, I cried inwardly, or quirk of fate has led me to buy this goddamned accursed Christ-bitten hotel anyway? Was I spawned to become a saloon keeper? So that my mother had me transfixed like a matador before the *quitte*. It is true that when I gave the man the check I was drunk. But in that rapturous moment when I looked over the bar at the silver footpath leading through the palm trees to the moon over Navy Island I had known I must call this bar mine. But did I, I cried out in torment, have to buy the whole goddamned hotel with its waiters, its cooking ranges, its ancient English old-school-tie guests, all so old they kept you awake at night dropping dead, thud, thud, thud?"

Errol's father had sharper reactions about that folly than his son. In a letter to me some time after Errol's death, he wrote of that venture: ". . . Any differences we had were due to the fact that to my mind he did not take sufficient care in the selection of some of the people he employed, e.g., he appointed a manager for the Titchfield Hotel who had failed in every job he had, including a period of hotel keeping. That little appointment cost Errol some £17,000 [$50,000]. Just at a time when he could least afford it."

The Titchfield was a two-story wooden hotel about fifty yards long. It had been built a long time before, perhaps a hundred years earlier, nobody actually knew when. The front of the hotel was given over to a bar that faced a swimming pool. Alongside the bar was a pavilion used for banquets, dances and entertainment. On one side of the hotel and angling out toward the bar was a dining area with round and square linen-covered tables and comfortable chairs. Across a channel of dark water was Navy Island, a spot of land that loomed a half mile away, green and unoccupied. Out beyond that rolled the Atlantic. All about the hotel were trees, trellises and bushes of tropical flowers; and at all times a breeze blew, bringing to those about the bar or the dining area wafts of tropic air.

If it was possible for a terrain, a locale to have gender, a male, female or neuter character, then the environs of Port Antonio and of this hotel, the Titchfield, were female. I got that feeling from the air, from the tropic warmth, from the water on all sides, dangerous, deep, yet inviting, as Errol found his women sometimes. There was an aura of licentiousness too: the old hotel with its thousand-times used beds occupied by travelers, lovers; the pool in front of the place where couples frolicked, where swimmers went about in casual undress; palm trees swinging in the steady breeze, and in the crotch of each palm bundles of coconuts, as on an orchard of virile males. Out beyond you could see nine miles of the Atlantic, the white, green and blue masses reflecting the sky—and in a moment a sudden downpour, like a woman crying mysteriously. Then once again hot sun all over, brightening everything.

A tempestuous female was this Jamaica: volcanic bush everywhere; burgeoning banana trees; birds of paradise cackling, nagging, howling up the air; insects believing they were God's gift to the biosphere, ruling everything; roaches tumbling in the grass, mosquitoes at home on the bar. Profligate, profligate all of it. No wonder the thought occurred to me, "Jamaica is a woman."

It was beautiful for playing, resting, even working. And this was the environment in which Errol wanted to do his book.

The work on his book began in a unique way. The first thing before we could even think of matters literary was a detail well the other side of sharpened pencils, a working typewriter, steno pads and the like. I was seated in his room waiting to get started when a retinue of four black men each carried through the door a case of vodka. They went out and returned a second time, each with another case of vodka. Eight cases, twelve bottles to the case. "That should get us part way through our Miltonesque operation," Errol intoned.

Williams, another dark-skinned Jamaican, came along a few minutes later bearing skin-diving paraphernalia. "Let's check the compressed air," Errol said. For about fifteen minutes there was a tangle of cord, air tubes and mechanism all over the floor and under the bed while Errol and Williams scrambled through it, untangling it and testing it. Errol discovered the compressed air tank was in bum shape. "They could be trying to kill me," he joked, "for which I wouldn't blame them." He gave directions for the repair of the tank. Williams scrambled out of the room with the same gear he had brought in.

We set up the working arrangement on a porch outside his second floor room. The stenographer, a black man, an expert court reporter, sat at a round table. Errol sat in a stiff-backed chair and I was nearby in a rocker.

I asked if he had any particular thing on his mind he wanted to start talking about. If so, that would be the place to begin. He thought he might like to begin somewhere near the beginning. "Most people think I'm an Irishman born in Ireland, by nature a cop, and we have to clear that up."

He wondered whether this talking-the-story-out technique could produce results.

I explained that writing one's own autobiography was an extremely difficult thing to do, that it was often better to talk it out and have a good questioner at hand.

As the morning progressed he acquired more of an affinity for the manner in which we worked, and he surmised, "I didn't know a job like this could be done this way."

In the succeeding days Errol opened up and there began to unfold the strangest of all stories: his first twenty-three or twenty-four years in "the lands down under." I listened in some bewilderment, realizing that I knew nothing about him. Neither did his public—if he were telling the truth, and I had no doubt all this was confessional and self-revelatory.

There issued from him an onrush, a spilling of his lifetime. I was surprised to learn that he was not at all an Irishman named Flynn from Ireland, as I and millions of others supposed from the Hollywood publicity, but that almost his entire formative period had been in Tasmania, Australia and New Guinea. Moreover, he was filled with unimaginable tales of a singular youthtime that exceeded, for adventure and strangeness, any role he had ever played on the screen, including *Robin Hood* and *Captain Blood.*

"What?" I said in incredulity, "you shot a native?" He gave me the details of a trial for murder in a New Guinea court. . . . "What? You were part of an underworld gang in Sydney, the Woolamaloo Gang?" . . . "What? You rounded up·aborigines and sold them as slaves for plantation labor?" . . . "What? You were a gold prospector in New Guinea at the Edey Creek Fields?" . . . He recounted a horrifying story of jungle nights, insects, malaria.

It went on like that for days, an outpouring that no man could imagine, so it had to be true. A lone white man in jungle country with spear-throwing aborigines.

Sometimes he told whole stories at one time, entire segments complete. But much issued in fragments, in hints of tales to come. I knew we would have to go back over all of this.

Most of the time we worked on that screened porch leading off his quarters. The traffic of the hotel went on. Dhondi moved in or out of the scene. Below, gardeners frittered with the lawn, snipped or cut: the rich scene of palm and tropic flowering waved like soft green breasts to the water's edge. Black hotel workers, mostly women, were inside dusting the rooms and murmuring to one another, "Fleen-Fleen!" They didn't exactly like him. He treated blacks, domestic help, very much in the tradition in which he had been reared in New Guinea—as serfs, a lesser species.

All of it was growing on me now, bit by bit: the man, the environment. I knew from the outset there was a secret corner in his development that pertained to his mother. I had gotten the clue to this at the airfield in New York when he spit out his rough characterization of her.

There was a certain terror in his telling. He sat opposite soaked in vodka as he unraveled; sometimes his hands chattered like leaves in a strong wind. I was looking at the end product of a man and his lifetime, and in a way what was pouring from him was his legitimate, his real bloodstream. Before me were two men: the finished creature who told his story and lived in Jamaica and the world in high hedonism, the one I whiled away the time with when we weren't at work on the book; and another, going back fifty years, whom I needed to understand in order to "put him together."

He tended to speak humorously, lightly, about most events in his life. He could tell a story when the joke was on him, and creativity was his essential ingredient. But it was only when he talked about his birth and growth in Tasmania, and his later experiences in New Guinea and Australia, that he seemed intent, serious. Ultimately I understood why. It was his origin, his childhood and adolescence, which was totally formative and also totally unknown to the moviegoing public. Nobody had ever believed him when he spoke of those events. Now he had a chance to set the record straight, so he was purposeful.

"It must have been a hard birth," he said of his appearance on June 20, 1909, "because it's been difficult with my mother ever since. Hard for her, hard for me."

Then, in this same vein, unsmiling, with something of ferocity in his telling, he came out with the tale of his life half a century earlier. . . .

He was born in Hobart, Tasmania, and christened Errol Leslie Thomson Flynn. His father was Theodore Thomas Flynn, a professor of marine biology. His mother, Marelle Young Flynn, was one of three daughters by a sea captain. It seems authentic and indisputable that the sea captain and his daughters were descended from Midshipman Young of the *H.M.S. Bounty*, that famous ship of the heralded mutiny.

The dour cold climate of Tasmania, a state in the Commonwealth of Australia, had something to do with the shape of Errol's future. Nothing much that happened on this island where he spent his first thirteen years endeared him to the memory of Tasmania itself. All about was sea and wilderness, and he loved the sea. But his mother, he said, was cruel to him. Or, as he put it, "Maybe I was too much to handle." For his childhood was sheer mother-son warfare.

From each parent he inherited an extraordinary aspect and capacity. His mother, a champion swimmer, was certainly beautiful. Her photograph, when she was young, holding Errol on her lap when he was five months old, discloses a stunning young woman. His father was a tall, regally erect man with the verve and vigor of all Ireland. Errol, shaped by his mother and the marine biologist father into some kind of sea serpent—he was at home early on or below water—swiftly acquired exceptional muscle, skin tone, build, growth. Very early, at seven, he was tough and independent enough to engage in a mutiny against his mother which, in a prismatic way, equaled the famed action of his forebear Midshipman Young against Captain Bligh.

The incident that set off the mutiny of the seven-year-old was his curiosity about the private zone of a pretty next-door neighbor of his age. Under a porch there were mutual examinations; they were caught. Errol was severely punished. He ran away from home, staying away three days, living hardily out in the open during that time "while looking for work."

Errol's relationship with his father was much more moderate. His father wasn't punitive with Errol, as was his mother. Errol went with him on exploration trips and watched him cut up sea specimens. But Errol was to suffer some benign neglect, the victim of his father's career.

When Errol was thirteen, Professor Flynn was asked to lecture at a few universities in England. Errol went to England with his parents. There he was dropped off at Southwest London College for two years. The crucial age was thirteen to fifteen. It was, said Errol, "a bum school." Nothing had changed since Dickens. Poor food, little word from his parents, loneliness. He teamed up with a hardy young Frenchman and together these two alienated ones held off the English students, who ribbed Errol because he was a "colonial."

Weekends, with an allowance of thirty-five cents, he walked to London. He beheld the great city, sensed the sweep and history of the place, and contrasted it with the simple, barren life of his faraway Tasmanian home. London, *this* was the real world, not Tasmania.

He didn't have "ambition" yet. He would get that later in New Guinea: ambition, dreams and a terrible need to "show the world" something, to "show his parents" something, to "show himself." But this period of isolation in the suburbs of London was an antipodal point in his development. He couldn't and didn't study. He was expelled at fifteen. Then expelled again from another English school.

The family returned to Sydney, Australia.

Errol now had a younger sister, Rosemary, age five when Errol was fifteen. He was placed in the select Northshore School, at Sydney, while Professor Flynn, Marelle and Rosemary went off to England again. Once more, abandoned. He was now a big, handsome fellow, a tough schoolyard fighter. Few in the school would bother to tangle with him.

Once more ejection from school, and Errol realized he

would have to make it on his own. He looked for work.

He got one job licking stamps, putting them on letters. He switched to another, an office job where he rifled the petty cash box: fired. And another stint, folding pamphlets for some radical political cause: short-lived. He was desperate now, so he and a companion named Thomson joined the Woolamaloo Gang. These were bandits capable of murder, and Errol pulled away from them after a week or so of association.

He was now seventeen, the year 1926. With the proceeds of an engagement ring he had given to a sweetheart named Naomi (she returned it to him) and some money borrowed from an uncle, he headed for New Guinea. There was gold there, other rich natural resources; it was untapped frontier.

This was our work scene: Errol sat a few feet away, his feet and legs propped up on a low table. In his right hand, almost unrelievedly, a tall glass of vodka. He sipped and talked, sipped again and talked again. At the other side of the table sat the young Jamaican taking shorthand. Very fast, very capable.

I think the starkest part of Errol's adolescent years was in that New Guinea experience. He was animated as he talked about it. He was reliving it before my eyes.

When Errol set foot on New Guinea it was one of the "darkest," most unexplored parts of the world.

Through being Professor Flynn's son he landed a post with the government service. He secured training as a cadet and became a constable, assigned to patrol the aborigine population and the handful of whites who had settled there.

Of a sudden he had status.

Photographs of him then show him dressed in white, with white helmet, carrying a walking stick, looking official, important and very British against the short, naked brown bodies of the New Guineans.

It took almost no time for Errol to be caught romancing a Polynesian girl who was married to a government official. As a result he was assigned to go deep into the interior of New Guinea to investigate the massacre of four Australian prospectors by jungle natives. Later he witnessed how the Australian government had several thousand New Guineans gather to watch the hanging of a band of natives, ostensibly to teach them all not to kill white men.

Fired from his job as a constable, he got another as overseer of a copra plantation at Kavieng, New Ireland: forty pounds a month. He directed the activities of a hundred native workers. Actually, a "boss boy" did the work of managing the New Guineans while Errol went about, cane in hand, tall, important, and useless but drawing his salary. It couldn't last long. Nothing ever could or would with Errol, not then, not later. (His longest-lasting arrangement was a stormy one with cinema king Jack Warner.)

For a time at Kavieng he was in the business of dynamiting fish. Then he was on the sea again, this time in the joint ownership of a schooner named the *Maski,* his partner a chap named Dusty Miller. They handled freight and occasional passengers about various New Guinea ports.

But at a crucial point in his arrangement he met a man who may have changed his life. Errol said the man's name was Joel Swartz. Swartz told Errol he wanted to film headhunters of the Sepik River. That river, six hundred miles long, ran halfway through New Guinea. Nobody knew its length, depth or nature—not even the natives. Errol called the river a human graveyard. It was a waterway replete with crocodiles, snakes, poisonous insects, poisonous shrubbery, the works.

I interrupted to ask, "How did you make out physically in all that brush and jungle?"

"I didn't. I picked up malaria, nearly died of it, and I get recurrences of it to this day. I'll have one for you before this research is done, you can bet. That disease alone was one of my main fears of staying there and an impetus to my getting out eventually. Also, at one of the ports I picked up the Pearl of Great Price," his euphemism for gonorrhea.

"Beyond these risks," he went on, "insect bites were incessant, often poisonous. I had fevers and deliriums traceable to some of these scratchy bites. You could be red from top to bottom from maggots, spiders, leeches, mosquitoes. They were in Flynn."

The film was supposed to be a travelogue but at the last Swartz confided to Errol that actually it was wanted by official sources in England and the United States. The authorities especially wanted shots of the river's mouth in the event there was ever trouble with the rising Japan.

While Errol guided the party up the Sepik the cameraman shot hundreds of feet of film of the region's flora and fauna, and of Errol disporting about the ship, the river, swimming. Willy-nilly he was in a film.

This later led to Errol being asked to play Fletcher Christian in an Australian film, *In the Wake of the Bounty,* released in 1933. Errol worked on it for three weeks for six pounds.

All agreed it was no great performance, but it was a beginning for the young adventurer.

There was talk of a gold strike around Edey Creek, a week's march from coastal Salamua. He sold his interest in the *Maski* to his partner, then made a rough journey into the New Guinea interior, going up and down mountainous ridges with a band of native guides to show the way. At last he found himself in the gold fields, but he wasn't about the region long: there was little gold, no women and great discomfort. Even so he staked a claim about a hundred yards square. Then he hastened back to Salamua, where he teamed up with another rough-and-ready type like himself, this one named Ed Bowen.

Bowen had a schooner, the *Matupi.* They wound up recruiting natives for plantation work. "Recruiting" was a euphemism for slave catching. In that dangerous pastime, Flynn, Bowen and their party found themselves in Dutch New Guinea territory, where they were attacked by natives. Errol shot and killed one in self-defense. He was arrested and tried for murder, but was acquitted.

From time to time money had come his way, small fortunes that he spent. One of them was a haul of five thousand dollars for the claim he had made at Edey Creek. His land was between two gold strikes. With that he bought a yacht, the *Sirocco.* He paid off a few debts and set sail with some friends on a three-thousand-mile trip up the coast of Australia. It was a tough voyage, and their ship barely made it. Errol said later in his book *Beam Ends,* which described that seven-month voyage, that there must be a kindly fate watching over foolish young men embarked on dangerous exploits.

Errol and his friends piloted the *Sirocco* into the harbor

of Port Moresby. He found the region especially green and beautiful; it was the rainy season. He looked over the resources of the area. Thirty miles away was the Laloki River, and Errol took a fancy to it. There he started a tobacco plantation. That is, native laborers built it at Errol's direction, and he went into the business of cultivating a tobacco estate. Tobacco growing was unknown thereabouts, but the use of tobacco was reaching the New Guineans, and Australia was a nearby ready market for the weed.

With his first profits he bought a beautiful girl, Tuperselai, from her Boss Boy father, a chap named Allaman: cost, two pigs, one fuse of English shillings and some seashell money. His time at Laloki was fairly idyllic compared with most of his New Guinea experiences.

When he slipped into his bamboo house at night after a day of horseback riding around his tobacco plantation he turned to books. He asked his father to send him Stevenson, Wells, the English poets, books of botany and biology; newspapers of the upper world, *The London Times*. Way down there in a country God Himself might despair of, with the sound of the *garramut* (war drums) in his ears and the *puk-puk* (crocodile) close by, and malarial insects on all sides, he went down into the well of his mother country's literature, and by hurricane lamp educated himself.

When Errol said to me, "There is no thrill like making a dishonest buck," I didn't know whether to believe him or not. But he meant it. Honest pay for an honest day's work? He had had that in the great array of curious jobs he held when he was seventeen and eighteen in Sydney. He found that honest work paid little. So, get over on the exploiting side of life, make others work for you. There was a ready reservoir for that approach: the aborigine population. You could buy them with salt and beads. He played the role of the colonial exploiter to the hilt and was honest enough to say so. Still, as he described these perfidies, portraying himself as a man of some wickedness, you could not dislike him. I could not. His tales were intriguing, splendid impossibilities out of an Alladin's Lamp of his own making—only the oil in it was real: a modern youth surviving for five years in Stone Age jungle country.

Port Moresby, Salamua, Sydney, Rabaul, Laloki, the deserts of Australia, altogether five years of foraging about the Australasian empire: fooling a native chieftain with a moneymaking machine, dagging the hogget (biting off sheep testicles, a job that went with the wool growing industry), anything to make a living.

It was evident by now that this was a young man in a terrible struggle for survival, living by his wits, his "natural advantages," his capacity for using his fists when needed, his ability to bluff his way through situations.

In his dreams he saw London again, the London he had visited when he was at that first school in the suburbs of the great city. This land below in the "Australasias," as it was then called in geography books, had to be abandoned. Get out. Go up there where the world was.

It was then he wrote letters to his father, who was alternately in Australia or London, saying he was fearful of being destroyed by New Guinea: malaria, which had already felled him, might kill him; natives might, anything might. He was in a whirl. Which way to turn: the law? writing? cinema?

He wrote that he hoped to go to England, study law, go up in British politics. Or perhaps turn to writing. He had already sold articles to the Sydney *Bulletin* on the life, practices and nature of the aborigines. Would his father help? There was no response from his father.

Errol knew that time was running out: there had been the slain native, his reputation as a slave recruiter. But he did have something to show for his time: fifty ounces of gold, four hundred pounds' worth, and a shaving brush filled with jewels he had stolen from an older sweetheart named Madge. The desperate hour arrived when he said to himself, "That's it, go home. Home where? Go to England. Leave this damnable jungle forever. You've got the money now, Flynn, get out!"

He made for the port of Rabaul. There, thanks to his father's name, he secured a passport.

At Rabaul he boarded a ship that would take him to Manila, out of that part of the world.

Between work sessions I found myself thinking about his early years. It was not so difficult to understand how, only a couple of years later, on board ship on his way to the United States, he could boldly walk up to the famous star Lili Damita and ask her to dance: and a bit later even marry her. The boldness, the guts, the raw force in him had been forged in those wild brutal years, out of the denial, the jungle, the loneliness, out of his own private vitals. So it was no wonder that within a year or two he burst upon the world scene as the most dashing figure alive.

On August 7 a Jamaican paper, *The Daily Gleaner,* carried an interview Errol initiated:

Film Star Errol Flynn is again on holiday in Port Antonio. He will remain at the Titchfield Hotel for the next month or so as he is here for a rest, and also to write his memoirs which his publishers are in a hurry to have published.

The publishers sent out Mr. Earl Conrad, one of their authors who has already published about 16 novels and many magazine stories, to collaborate in the writing of the story. Mr. Conrad is accompanied by his secretary.

He returned from Africa via New York and from there he flew down with Mr. Conrad.

He said, "Jamaica is for me more and more, apart from the job I am doing now, where one can work and have fun. The itinerary —morning work, mid-day drinking, afternoon exercise, evening a bit more drinking, and then to bed." That, he said, is a fair day in the tropics.

Turning to local conditions since last he was here, he said he feels he is a part of this country and is sad that more is not done for this end of Jamaica. He has decided that he will have to do something himself particularly for the people in the Boston district where he has his holdings. He will devote some of his money which is not tax free in building what he thinks is the urgent requirement in that particular district.

He also intends to start a pension scheme for his employees working on his estates as he wants to see their children benefited and that would also be one way of attracting the best employees for the estates.

I had no idea he was philanthropic. This part of Jamaica, the north end, seemed to me to be indeed a poor part of the world. Only one fourth of the people wore shoes because only one fourth could afford them. The people looked lean; there was a large-scale dental problem among

I decided: that is one fine thing that Errol wants to help.

I had no doubt I was associated with a man of great integrity as to communities of people—although with time I noticed that the only occasion in which he ever mentioned the word integrity was when he referred to whorehouses as "places of special integrity."

But all this, his philanthropic plan, pension and all, awaited its season a few weeks hence.

Here Errol had a heated tussle with Dhondi. She complained that he was paying all of his attention to the book and little to her.

"That's right!" he roared. "I'm paying a helluva lot of attention to my book! Twenty-four hours a day and I'm going to keep on!"

They seemed deliberately to hurt each other: an old theme in love affairs.

Dhondi had a limited understanding of what an autobiography might mean to a man like Errol, now forty-nine, world rover, cashing in his chips perhaps, anxious to do a great work, especially as he was deeply frustrated. He saw in his book a chance for recovery of his earliest and strongest ambition—which was to be a writer. He knew he had a big story.

No, the book was Number One!

That feud, young feline jealousy over a man's other interest, simmered throughout the summer. She wanted one hundred percent attention.

No woman ever secured that from Errol Flynn.

After the newspaper article word went about Jamaica that Errol Flynn had come in: a signal for tourists, gapers, fans, sightseers to trek to the Titchfield long enough to see him in the flesh, and in the case of many of the females hopefully to have an affair with him. I was intrigued to learn how many women were willing and anxious to lift themselves out of a fantasy life into the real thing.

A forty-year-old woman, tall, handsome, brunette, full of charm and pleasantly voiced, appeared at the bar only a few days after we arrived. She learned that I was an aide of sorts to Errol and promptly told me that she had flown in from Miami in hopes of meeting him. She had a son, she said, who looked like Errol, and so she very much wanted to know the actor. Could I help?

"You stay here at the bar," I suggested. "Errol and I will be lunching soon. You can keep an eye on us while I do what I can. For the rest you'll be on your own."

She pressed my hand thankfully.

At luncheon I told Errol where to take a look. "Her son looks like you," I explained.

He glanced her way. "She's a good looker, isn't she?"

"Beautiful," I said.

"Not my type," he promptly announced. "That's my type," and he pointed to a nymphet about fifteen who had been hanging about the hotel for many hours trying to get Errol's attention, not being forestalled in the slightest that Dhondi, with some ostensible claim on Errol, was already in the picture. I learned that women interested in him didn't give a damn about one another and weren't fazed by wives, mistresses, law, protocol, fences, mad dogs or anything else.

"I'll talk to her," said Errol, looking in the brunette's

direction, "since she's come all the way from Miami, but that's all."

After luncheon he drifted over to the bar. He invited the lady to a table, bought her a drink, kept an amiable conversation going for half an hour. There it ended.

Errol had too much on his mind these days: the book, diving equipment that wasn't working well, Dhondi, me, and now that other blonde nymphet who seemed to be peering about corners at him in a shy (not too shy) Peter Pan fashion.

He had looked at her once, long enough to let her know he had noticed her, then whispered to me, "That'd take me about two days."

"Two days?" I echoed. "All that time? I'm sure two hours'd do it, Errol."

"Oh no, you can't do it that way," he said. "Not unless you're buying it outright. These are fans, sweethearts, women you don't have to pay for. They have seen me on the screen and they've passed beyond their fantasy life into trying a direct confrontation. They have imagination. What they want is a little romance: some sweet talk, a bit of gentle fondling, a workup, something to remember the situation by. It doesn't have to be too much, but some dalliance. Eye-work. There has to be something to remember.

"When the moment is right," he added, with the devil in his eye, "you plunge into the mattress."

Still, I was to discover in succeeding weeks that romances of this sort weren't all that welcome or necessary to him. They came to him too easily. He had only to appear on the scene anywhere and ripe flowers grew about him, expecting him to light upon them like a bumblebee seeking pollen, and they anticipated providing the pollen.

He had other game. The other game did something for him that the light romances did not.

The black girls of Jamaica. They were brought to the hotel by one of his dark-skinned pimps. The girls would stand in the driveway as he assayed them. He looked down at them from the second-story porch on which we worked. He would pick one or another of possibly two or three girls brought along to be looked over by him. The chosen one would be called upstairs and perhaps not be with him for more than five or ten minutes.

About the hotel nobody much noticed the conduct of the transaction. I myself grew indifferent to these brief siesta-deals that occurred in so public a way. Usually at noon. The girls stood below, the pimp ascended the stairway and went into Errol's quarters; then pimp and Errol stood on the porch and looked down. Errol beckoned, "You—tall one— come up—show me good time."

A few times when we finished work, Errol and I strolled in the Port Antonio market square or to some pub. The idea was simply to walk about, see what was doing, then go back to the hotel.

Tradesmen would be moving about. An occasional impoverished prostitute would be plying her trade.

Once he saw a handsome statuesque light-colored girl and beckoned to her. She came across the street to his side.

"I need a nurse. Do you know how to nurse?" He wasn't sure she was in the life. She might be just a Jamaica girl walking by.

The young woman said, "Dem make good nurse, Mr. Fleen."

"Dem" is a word used in Jamaica to mean just about everything and everybody: all genders, all things.

Errol propositioned: "Me needing nurse. Pay you good. Two pounds a week." That, at the time, was about five bucks, top salary for a week in Jamaica for domestic work, a nurse, secretary, cook, most any service performed by a female. Males were paid about the same.

She may have "nursed" him only once or twice and discovered he was perfectly well.

After noting Errol's habits at the outset, I paid little attention to what was happening. Observing that this was a feature of his daily experience like eating or dressing or shaving, I said to myself, "That's Flynn. He's at it all the time." Inwardly I shrugged.

It was difficult for me to see in him anything other than a total male constantly at work. He often remarked, "I'm probably oversexed." In his case he could consummate the full energy he felt: he had the money, the time, the reputation, the gall to make good at it daily.

While indulging himself with females, he also indulged all day in hard drink—whiskeys, rum, vodka—and also in swimming, boating, skin diving, work—all with the same vigor and always incessant. I have never seen anyone else who had his constancy of emotional and physical expenditure.

It was simply Errol Flynn alive and breathing and living it up even beyond the public image of himself.

Between work sessions he planned fun and trips about North Jamaica. He was always working on what he called "a fair day in the tropics."

In his love for Jamaica and the ocean around it, the Rio Grande River, the volcanic jungle, he had returned to the scenes of his youth. The trap that he had fled in his early twenties he now sought out. Nostalgia had come over him. He moved his arm deftly, waving at the mountainous jungle that spread and rose out beyond Port Antonio. "This is like Central Africa," he said. He had recently returned from Africa, where he appeared in *Roots of Heaven.* He motioned down the Rio Grande River, a narrow fast-running murky stream. "It's like the Sepik." Like the Sepik in New Guinea where he had shot a native, where the Stone Age people went about with bows and arrows, with poisoned spears. Here in Jamaica it wasn't much different, only more mechanized, modernized. The blacks moved about barefooted. Everyone wore sunbonnets, for the intense overhead sun beat on everybody. Errol went about sweating and sweltering as he had once done on the copra plantation he managed near Port Moresby. All of it was recollection. Pretty black girls went about barely clad, as did the black natives of Laloki. The people here had a kind of pidgin English too; a Calypso English that whites couldn't follow or speak. Errol couldn't.

When a young girl aged thirteen came by with her mother, the mother carrying on her head a large bundle of clothes, they recognized the great Fleen and smiled. Errol looked at the girl and said, "Lif up, lif up!" The girl raised her shirtwaist over her head, her beautiful black torso and small lovely breasts exposed for his approval. She was smiling, three teeth in front missing.

Why Errol found it necessary to talk "pidgin English" to the natives of Jamaica I never understood. I never had any difficulty making myself clear by talking New York English. I found prompt comprehension on all sides.

But Errol had a way of curtailing his sentences sometimes. He thought he was miming the Jamaicans' sub-English and he believed they understood him better. I think it was merely a reversion to the pidgin English he used in New Guinea where it must have been necessary.

Jamaica was an echo for him of his adolescence, and he slipped into pidgin English on a kind of romanticized return trip to Laloki.

Everything here was less expensive, one fourth the cost of living in the United States. "Like Spain," he said to me, where he had his sailboat, the *Zaca,* anchored. "You can live in Spain at one fourth the cost of living in the States." (Errol, who had gone through millions, much of it taken from him, was as cautious about economy as anyone, cautious within the framework of a certain carelessness.)

It was all a touch of the past that had staged and framed him in an earlier era and that he was reliving.

"We'll go fish on the Rio Grande today," he said.

I knew that meant he would take along his spear, his diving equipment. He would go below fifteen or twenty feet, toss his spear at something or other, then come up, exercised.

"We'll catch the big snook today," he said, giving me a sly look.

"The snook? What is it?" I asked, thinking it was like a bass, a trout, a perch, a shark or some other fish.

"We'll catch it one of these days," he answered, a wry smile over his face as he busied himself with his diving equipment.

I began to look forward to its capture. All that I knew of fish in the river were a few piddling ones about eight inches long.

"The big snook," he repeated. "Yes, the big snook."

•   •   •

Errol, in his own way, with his limitations, excesses and emotional paradoxes, was in love with Dhondi. She was a bright moment in his climactic days.

He got a charge out of Dhondi's naïveté. If he mentioned Aristotle she dashed back at him, "Who's this Harry Tottle?" He loved that.

He said, "Don't give me peremptory orders." She rushed to the dictionary, found out she had been abrupt and bossy with him, and promised not to be "premtery" with him ever again.

It was all refreshing fun to him, a little like having one of his daughters around, except he was entitled to take this one to bed.

Meantime his fancy turned elsewhere. . . .

Errol cultivated physicians. He needed them frequently for legitimate illnesses which beset him and for intelligent companionship.

On the third evening of our arrival Dr. Tom Lawrence came around to see Errol and say hello. Not more than ten or fifteen minutes passed when Errol pulled the same thing on the doctor as he had with me at the airport hotel, calling his mother a cunt.

The doctor was as unsettled as I had been. What the hell was Errol's game?

I studied both of them.

I was learning that Errol liked to shock, to be outrageous, to study the reactions of people when he had unsettled them. He liked playing games with other people's emotions. At the same time, he did have a bitter lifetime feud with his mother that I still knew little about.

Thereafter, from time to time. Dr. Lawrence came by

with his beautiful young wife. They were usually evening visits for half an hour or so. The doctor was about forty-five, his wife half his age. The physician ministered to Errol's medical needs and the wife helped Errol's eyes. Her name was Athene. Errol confided to me that he had never seen anyone in Hollywood more attractive, more physically animated or more proportionally perfect. He ran off a list of names of famous screen beauties, saying not this one, not that one, not Paulette, not Lana, not Carole, not any other.

"I must sample that," he told me with a certain urgency, challenging me to note how he would go to work.

In the succeeding days Errol pursued his objective. The couple came to the hotel frequently and we went boating with them. I was charmed by the friendliness and intelligence of each.

"Migods, Errol," I said, "she seems a perfectly happy girl and the doctor a perfectly happy guy. They live quiet lives here in Port Antonio. Look, you don't have to prove anything to me. I don't doubt your superb talent."

"I've got to have her," he said. "I'm not thinking of you or the book or anything in the world. I have to see what that's like."

He turned to a piece of paper on a table. "Did you see what Athene was doodling on this paper when she was last here?"

I hadn't noticed she was doodling or doing anything but looking at him with some interest because he was the great actor. Everybody looked him over that way.

"Take a look at this."

I looked at a patch of pencil markings on the back of an envelope. I couldn't make a thing out of it.

"That's a snatch," he said.

"A snatch?" I repeated. I took another look at it. Yes, it did look like pubic hair and a line down through it.

"That's what's on her mind," he exclaimed. "I've already talked to her."

"Really?"

"Yes, I've promised to put her in pictures—if she *will.*"

"What did she say?"

"Nothing yet."

"What does Doc Lawrence think of it?"

"He doesn't know yet."

The next time the physician appeared I thought he looked a bit distressed, as if something of the situation had already been conveyed to him. Then, from the side, I listened as Errol tried to convince the doctor that he should take Athene to Hollywood. "She will absolutely be the greatest actress. She's got the looks, she's smart, she has the manner. I can make an actress out of her in no time. We can do this kind of thing back there, you know."

He was giving this poor husband as hard a line as a pharmaceutical salesman pushing a new chemical cure-all. He had his arms around the man, urging, persuading. He was doing this for the doctor as well as for Athene. They would be wealthy, she would be famous. "She will cut out a whole new career for herself," he argued.

"But Errol," said the doctor, trying to hang onto his bit of happiness, "I'd rather we didn't do anything like that at all. Why don't we just let her stay here in Jamaica with me?"

"Thomas, Thomas! You are being gauche and I am surprised at you. Here you are keeping something from the world. She deserves to be seen by everybody."

"But Errol," pleaded the poor harassed M.D., who never

expected that his friend was going to come up with any such proposition, "I don't even believe Athene wants to do this."

"Believe me, she will."

Errol's arms were still around the doctor. He was gentle, soft, it was all being done in the name of good creative art, for the world of art, for the benefaction of the human race. She must become a famous actress.

"How can you do this to me?" Errol implored, as if he were the affronted one.

"I know I'm being hard on you, Errol," said the gentle doctor, truly a good doctor, "but I rather think not now. Not at this time. Please!"

The whole deal ended then and there. Athene never left Jamaica.

What stayed within me was again having heard him speak of his mother by that four letter word—this time to the respectable doctor.

Though I set about delving into Errol's relationship with his mother, nothing definitive appeared in *My Wicked, Wicked Ways* beyond his own assertions that his lifetime feud with her continued into the present. With time I have a better view of it. . . .

Errol's practice with females has to be explicable largely in terms of his personal origins—the war with his mother. He had told the story of some childhood play beneath a porch with a little girl named Nerida. It had gotten well through the "show me" stage when Nerida's mother caught them. Nerida was simply told she mustn't do that, but Errol received a serious thrashing from his mother. She made him feel that what he did was indescribably ugly. She tried to force him to tell his father, but Errol was so chastened he couldn't talk to his father. His mother called him "a dirty little brute."

She instilled in him the thought that sex, the genitals, were sinful. He received from that baptism a fear and a confusion, plus an abnormal concern about sex. Moreover, that incident had been preceded by continuous clashes with his mother in which he was repeatedly whipped.

Something had to have been going on there between mother and son. Whatever it was, it colored his entire life, had much to do with his regard and alternately disregard of females; it had much to do with his several marriages, much to do with his satyriasis, if that's what he suffered from. He both needed and rejected females all the days of his life.

He has told the story one way, his mother another.

She, in a letter to me, described Errol's early days this way:

Dear Mr. Conrad:
As a child, as a baby even, Errol always loved to dress up & act the part—actually living the part, as one day, when staying with my parents, I had taken him for a walk & he was playing trains, when we met an old friend of the family, to whom I was glad to proudly show my little son. To my surprise Errol would not speak —he who usually had everything in the world to say. Later, when the man had passed, I asked him why he would not speak, and he answered, "Doesn't he know that trains cannot speak?" I said, "Of course, but he doesn't know that you were a train." "Well, then," said Errol, "he is very stupid." He was then only about 2½ years old. That was a remarkable thing about Errol, the extraordinary long words he used & his little grown up manner of speaking—which was extremely funny & used to make me die of laughter. On another occasion, we were invited to a tea party on a

Japanese warship. I decided to take him too, knowing he would like to see a warship. The headmaster of his preparatory school was there—Errol was about six at the time. I said to Errol, "Aren't you going to speak to Mr. So and So (I've forgotten the man's name). Errol replied, "No, mummy, as a matter of fact I'm avoiding him." I, highly amused at such a reply, asked why & was told, "Well, if I speak to him he is sure to enter into a long conversation with me." This sort of speech made me sure he was going to be a great writer—and I still am of that opinion—had he only applied himself to writing seriously. He started by having articles published in the Sydney *Bulletin*—no small achievement, I assure you.

He ran away once from home when he was about seven & we suffered agonies of anxiety for days & nights. He was found miles away where he went & offered himself for work at a dairy farm. He asked only 5/ a week as wages, saying that would do him as he "never intended to marry." As a little boy he was the most delightful little fellow one could meet but such a wee fickle that he had constantly to be watched. Another time we missed him. He had gone fishing for the goldfish in the ornamental pond of the city square. Another time on a ship, I missed him out of my cabin & ran up on deck & to my horror saw him standing on the taffrail being Neptune apostrophizing the waves—one lurch of the ship & he would have been overboard before I could grab him.

Ever yours,
Marelle Flynn

After he was famous, she and the professor arrived in New York and met the press, and when the reporters asked her how she felt about her son's fame, she told them, "He was a nasty little boy."

A lifetime row, as he said. No getting together, misunderstanding over every detail. So the war began in infancy, from the time he could toddle.

Marelle Flynn was a woman of strong personality, determined self-belief, with a sense of discipline and urgency about her son which she never let him forget. The evidence is that he was escaping her clutches from the earliest days and she was possessing him as seriously as he was seeking to escape that possession.

Where did she get her ideas of child-rearing and discipline? From those seagoing ancestors of hers: flogging, the brig, Coventry, obedience? All of those purported virtues of the British Navy circa the time of the *Bounty?* Some of this did spill over into her child-rearing proclivities. She didn't know how to contend with that bundle of energy except by flogging, the slap across the thigh or buttock, the incessant *don'ts.*

In a subsequent note to me, Marelle Flynn spoke of the tradition among her forebears of illicit "blackbirding" (enslaving natives), of the British government being sent out to punish natives who fought the inroads of adventurers. It was not difficult to sense the naval influence, the discipline, the overarching rigidity. Had this approach been part of Marelle Flynn's handling of her son? The likelihood seemed strong to me as I read:

. . . Amongst Errol's forebears were many adventurous types, men of spirit who left the confines of English provincial life to start anew in Canada & Australia. Amongst these men were two brothers, Robert & Frederick Young, who with their patrimony bought themselves a schooner, the Heather Belle, & sailed it to the South Seas to trade. At that time "blackbirding" was taking place, that is, capturing the natives from the islands & selling them to work on the sugar plantations of Queensland. This of course was against the law, & Government ships were sent to patrol these seas. When a "blackbirder" found himself in danger of being overhauled & his ship examined, if he had any contraband cargo aboard, he would simply open the hold & put the unfortunate natives overboard, callously letting them drown. With the result that all ships were held in great suspicion by the islanders, and reprisals were taken wherever possible. When the brothers Young arrived in Sydney they parted company, Frederick taking his share of the ship in money with which he bought property, settled & married & became Errol's great grandfather. Robert, with the Heather Belle, went trading in the South Seas. Whether he was engaged in blackbirding was never proved. However he arrived at a certain island, was invited ashore by the Chief to trade. He being the owner & Captain of the ship was the first to land, was immediately set upon & murdered by the natives. The others in the same boat escaped back to the ship but through their glasses they saw the body of Robert put on a bier, a great fire made & dances & a cannibal feast took place. For this the British Government sent a gunboat to punish the natives, & their villages were shelled & destroyed.

Errol became bitter about his mother and in a manner of speaking, he went through life fighting her through fighting the world, insulting and hating the world as he inwardly insulted and hated his mother—yet admiring the physical beauty of the world even as he recognized the physical beauty of his mother. There is an old expression: the apple does not fall far from the limb.

Psychologists have observed that a child frequently whipped or disciplined or even abused by a parent may retain close lifelong attachments to the abusing parent.

Errol was reared in a sharply conventional home: his mother had a streak of Church of England within her and tried to pass it on to her son while the son picked up from his father Darwinism, agnosticism and a sense of to hell with it all, as far as religious absolutes were concerned.

Marelle Flynn must have had similar social-sexual conflicts. She wound up heavily in the arms of Christ, but in her younger days, Errol said, she was a merry one around Paris while her husband probed the oceans in search of marine biology findings.

His mother left a few of her trademarks upon him: they recurred in his conversations from time to time as he applied his own wrath to others as she had to him. She used the word "whaff" when she whacked him around; it was his favorite term for making someone toe the line. She who loved water and the outdoors often said to him when he was small, "Let's get out in the sun." He used the expression frequently.

Finally, when he said or did something his mother didn't like, she said in a withering way, as the English and the Aussies do, "Pity."

When Errol said, "Pity," if something didn't go the way he liked, it was like a histrionic utterance. It came out with a snakelike length, "Pittttttt-eeeeeee." And by the time the receptor caught the last "e" he was withered.

We all have to learn our ways and manners from somewhere or invent them, and Errol had a good tutor at home.

Pittttttt-eeeeeee!

All that might sound negative, as if his mother had no positive bearing upon him. Not true. She was the great water influence in his life, perhaps more so than his male parent, the marine biologist. She taught him to become a specie of human fish, allowed him to so develop. This interest and avocation became one of the great recourses of his existence. He felt some enormous indebtedness to his mother, who made him understand the beauty of water.

A great swimmer when she was young, she took him into

the water with her whenever she went to the beach. He moved easily over and under water, and she let him have a fish's freedom. She cultivated his at-homeness there and she told him that he was a descendant of Midshipman Young of the revolt on the *Bounty*. There were seafaring figures in the Young family: he met them when they visited Hobart. Out of this came his early fascination with sailboats, sea travel, captaining his own vessels, the *Maski*, the *Sirocco*, later the *Zaca*.

It is no wonder he felt bound to the woman from whom he was bound to revolt. The debt was too great.

It was like mother, like son: an attachment of fire and water.

There was an unmistakable mother-son influence between them that was gyroscopic: from her to him and from him back to her. That was in some large part the essential Errol, the one who became famous and then behaved as he did: rich, unhappy, roistering, thoughtful, experienced . . . and desolate.

Tasmania was the nursery for it all.

His war with his mother continued right through the writing of the book in Jamaica.

Errol wrote to his parents asking their help in providing some early recollections. He also asked me to write to them, which I did. His father replied directly saying, "I will also do what I can although our current opinions of Errol would burn up any paper on which they were written."

On October 28, 1958—we were deep into the research —Marelle Flynn wrote to me from St. Albans, Hertz, England, saying:

I am rather at a loss how to proceed with the material you required for Errol's book. I was going on with what you asked me to do. Now Errol writes to his father that he does not require anything from me. So what am I to do? I am sorry that there has been some misunderstanding, but as I told you, I was quite willing to cooperate to the best of my ability.

With the kindest regards,

Yours ever,
Marelle Flynn

It wasn't until two years after Errol's death that I learned why there was special friction between parents and son at the time we were writing the book. Errol had stopped off in England on his way back from making *The Roots of Heaven* in Africa. With him was fifteen-year-old Dhondi, who had been with him in Africa. The parents were outraged to behold their son cavorting about the globe with one so young. Professor Flynn wrote to me, "I was mad that Errol should have put himself in danger of another trial for statutory rape. Both of them told me lies with regard to her age."

It was, of course, a reasonable anxiety. Neither the son nor his parents ever got over the scandal and impact of his 1942–43 trial for alleged statutory rape in Los Angeles.

Here he was again, an older man, in his late forties, romping about the sphere with a fifteen-year-old. He hadn't learned a thing, his parents feared; and a whole new legal eruption might occur. Now, sixteen years later, Errol, as if in defiance of his fate, undertook a reenactment of the early experience with an underage girl—but this time openly for the whole world to see and note.

Errol was still a couple of weeks away from telling me about that statutory rape case.

•   •   •

Errol's prospects for the next few weeks were what might be called shipshape: visits to his estate, water trips, an upcoming horse racing event, a trip to Port Maria to see his friend Hannah Rixmann. Any day now his sister Rosemary would fly in from Washington, D.C., to help on the book. Maybe we would take a weekend drive way up into the hills of the Blue Mountains, four thousand feet high, where the coffee grew. "Magnificent view of the world from there," he promised—if we went.

Rest, real rest, was unknown to him.

From the day our plane arrived in Jamaica, Errol kept telling us that we would make a trip to Boston Estate. "I have to ride my ranch," he said. I built visions of him on horseback, like a cowboy, ranging over flat ground, perhaps with a Southwest American-style mesa in the background, as he counted cows. Hadn't he made Westerns?

Actually he had several hundred cows on his estate, supposedly the best in Jamaica, he said. Their bones showed much less than the bones on other cows you saw on other acreage. Cows didn't do well on Jamaica pasturage.

Boston Estate was what the Flynn acreage was called. It was a vast copra plantation stretching for miles along a jungle-encased road. Most of the land was covered with well-groomed, well-placed coconut trees. Errol told me his land might be worth one or two million—he didn't know how much as prices were going up. On that estate he had caretakers and plantation hands who picked limes and other citrus, cared for the cows, took care of a makeshift racetrack he had there and looked after horses that looked mangy, chickens, hogs, goats and almost anything else that crawls, flies or walks and could be found around a Jamaica plantation.

Once there we would have a chance, at Boston House, the center of the estate, to taste some of his mother's pimento wine. From the time he had first seen the island in 1947 and decided that this was to be his home and begun buying land along the north shore, his parents had alternated between living at Boston House and commuting to their place in the suburbs of London. On the estate, he said, his mother made the wine, was active in local church affairs and swam a lot in the nearby ocean waters.

I anticipated all this as something special; so did Dhondi.

One day the three of us, chauffeured by one of Errol's aides in a ramshackle limousine hired for the occasion, set out for a ride of twelve miles alongside the Rio Grande River, which stemmed away from Port Antonio into the jungle interior. "When you begin to see blue fences, that's my estate," he said.

On the way I discovered what a poetic response Errol had to nature. He pointed out feelingly the beauties of the hillsides; they were lush and rich in color as they receded backward and upward into a horizon of treetops. There was a sensate green everywhere: greens and brilliant yellows, and all kinds of plant life I couldn't identify. We drove for a time along the river, then up a hillside on a bumpy asphalt road for miles as the smell of jungle warmth and the color of the curling bushes intensified.

The blue fences began and soon we saw an entranceway on which was a sign, BOSTON HOUSE. The driver turned in through a winding trail, we climbed, and at last stopped before a not very pretentious old place. It was a wooden house, the outside weather-beaten. Bushes and trees obscured it. Vines crawled over the porches and up the windows.

When we stopped black faces peered from behind fences and trees. A dozen people came forward to greet the great man returned from Africa and the rest of the world. They hadn't seen him in ten months.

Errol showed me around in back. There were huts, pens and coops scattered here and there. I had the feeling that it was southern Alabama, year 1832. A family had the use of the estate in return for caring for Boston House. They foraged off the soil and the hills, ate the sulphurous-tasting eggs of Jamaica, *teefed* the coconuts and the breadfruit from the nearby trees.

Louise, a pretty black woman in her thirties, was mistress of the place. When she had shaken hands with Errol and with us, she said, "What I bring dem? Pimento wine? Vodka? Ice? What I bring dem?"

"Pimento wine, my mother's wine," Errol ordered. And he explained, "My mother [I was glad to hear him use that word] makes this wonderful wine. There ought to be a barrel of it down in the cellar. Jamaica is the only place in the world where the pimento grows." He turned to Louise. "I hope there is ice, Louise. Plenty of ice."

"Oh yes, Master Fleen, dem plenty of ice, because we knowing you back on the island, and we even has ice in the box when you not here, because we know you might fly in any time and we never without ice."

We sat on the porch, looking out at the Caribbean, studying the insects that hovered over the bushes, the ants that crawled over the porch table, breathing in the scent of frangipani, orchid and other flowers. New York seemed far away and I didn't miss it.

Children were off to the side watching us. A mangy dog curled on the staircase and scratched. The insects regarded dogs as the fairest game of all. All over Jamaica the dogs were bleeding pulps. Something had happened to the metabolism of the island; there were few animals but insect life roared and droned like airplanes near a hangar.

I went inside to browse around the living room. A library of books about biology spread across one wall: they seemed old, used, mastered by Professor Flynn. An unusual and valuable collection, I thought.

It had been well worthwhile, waiting to get out to Boston House. And now the pimento wine made by Errol's mother was served to us. Errol poured it into tall glasses and added chunks of ice.

The adult Jamaicans had retreated somewhere into the background. They had seen the master and now, politely, they dropped out of sight while he and his guests enjoyed their drinks on the porch. The company, they knew, would be around only a short while.

Louise kept bringing fresh trays of the rapidly melting ice. I wondered where the ice came from in this tropic quarter of the world.

Inside the house I took a look at the icebox. It was small, but a luxury for Jamaica. In the box were twenty-five or thirty pounds of ice, sure enough, and bottles being kept cool all around it.

We weren't there more than an hour. The fun wore off, the excellent wine wore off, the sight of the broad Caribbean began to pall.

There was one certitude I had: that at the center of our trip to Boston House was that icebox and the ice within it. The people around the place lived to nurse that icebox year-round so that it would be ripe and ready and cool when the master returned from his global exploits long enough to stay there an hour, look at the ocean, take a glass of pimento wine and be gone.

Back at the Titchfield that evening Errol put in a phone call to his attorney, the Honorable Vincent Grosset, who lived nearby. He was judge, lawyer and friend.

In the evening Vin, as Errol called him, came by the hotel, and in Errol's room I listened to his latest plans.

"Vin, I am going to give up Boston House and I want Louise and her whole family to get out. I am building a new house at Castle Comfort."

"All of them, now?" Vin asked. He was a middle-aged man, mustachioed and light-complected, with a pleasant subservient manner.

"Yes, they must all get out. I won't be able to afford to keep the house. I am building this new one and there'll be no need for that house."

"Louise has been with you a long while, ever since you arrived here."

"I know. She will have to go."

"Where will they go?"

"That is their problem."

"When do you wish this taken care of?"

"Right away."

"Whatever you say, Errol."

There was a silence.

Outside the window the evening sun had set very rapidly. It had gotten low in the sky, and as suddenly it was gone and there was a star-filled horizon.

The lawyer asked if there was anything else that he needed to know.

Ah yes, Errol did think of one thing. Though the family

would go, the house would be unoccupied for some time till he disposed of it. He might wish to make another visit out there to taste some of his mother's pimento wine.

"On second thought, Vin," he said, giving his lawyer an intent look, "save one man for the ice."

Had I heard right? Of course I had.

Out there, on lonely days and during lonely nights, one black serf would stay in a hut behind Boston House, and each day he would go into "the big house" and see how the ice was or have more ice delivered, whatever the task required. He would watch that ice patiently week after week, month after month, until the master returned from Hollywood or New York once more for an hour's visit to Boston House—and a cool drink.

You see, Earl, I said to myself later, you are nothing. You are nobody and you'll never be anybody. Here is Flynn, world famous, revered, powerful, with thousands of acres of coconuts and his picture a pinup in girls' rooms all over the world for a generation. Here is a man. You, Earl, are nothing and you will never have a dime. You'll never be able to turn to your lawyer, as did Errol, and dispose of the lives of twelve people and airily say, "Save one man for the ice."

Soon afterward he began building his new house at Castle Comfort, a luxury home costing a hundred thousand. It would overlook his property and stand like a private elaborate lighthouse of his own from which he could look at the Atlantic he loved so well.

I met contractors, house designers: people came and went.

I heard talk of insurance on the ancient house a distance

away which his parents from time to time occupied. His parents were now in England. Ostensibly they, like Errol, would be occupying the new home whenever they wished to spend time in Jamaica.

Unlike the famed Venetian Casanova, the gambler-adventurer-writer whose *Memoirs* boast of his feminine conquests (critics and students of that life suggest his boasts may have been in large part mythical), Errol's record of his relationships (in case the Guiness World Records people are interested) is there in his letters, his marriages and divorces, his children by various marriages, his whorehouse exploits, his assignations with women of virtually every color, nationality and class in the world.

Legendary tales of his sexual prowess travel up and down and across the country to this day, but the record is there in his autobiography, in letters written to him, and in much else that is documented, including the court records of the City of Los Angeles. And my own daily vigils with and about him.

"I had a vasectomy," he told me, "because I was going broke trying to pay the way for my ex-wives and kids." With that bit of surgery he could indulge to his heart's content and not worry; but he didn't get around to that until late in his career.

He was honest enough to wish to be reported as he actually was, as he had been most of his days, and as he was at the time of our joint venture in 1958 when he was forty-nine years old.

When he told me of one of his "passages," a curiously out-of-date expression for a sexual union, he said, "I told the young lady, 'Let me disillusion you right away about the size of my friend down here.' "

This time, as he described how he had not misrepresented himself to that female, he flashed his phallus before me. He was agile about opening his fly, buttons or zipper no matter. Sheer speed: and his air was always one of fun, never salaciousness. His penis was indeed unremarkable. It was, if not short, certainly not much longer than that, and rather stout, I thought. That's all there was, there wasn't any more, except a terribly full, bulging scrotum.

I had seen the original often. Many about the town of Port Antonio and the island of Jamaica saw that phallus. For Flynn carried himself generally with an openness that belied any undue restraint or modesty in that quarter. Many of us saw him often, in the evening, at the swimming pool of the Titchfield losing his shorts in the pool. At any time five or ten persons might get a view of his athletic but out-of-repair form and his genitals, and nobody gave it a thought. That was Flynn, do-as-you-please Flynn. He didn't overdo it, and he didn't do it for effect, but if he happened to lose his swimming trunks while giving the pool a good go, or in getting out of it, to hell with it. He trotted over to his towel and was soon—shall we deliver ourselves of this one—decent.

Often in the morning when I knocked on his door and asked if he were ready to start work, he would call me in, tumble out of bed, walk about in the nude (like the late President Johnson or Winston Churchill), head for the bathroom, and his member—stupid term, forgive me for running out of synonyms—his member would be tossing about shriveled, careless, indifferent or tired.

It was difficult to associate this central detail with his vast international reputation and his spiritual-psychical descent from Don Juan and Casanova.

"You can't do it in the water," he mourned sadly. He

Errol, aged five months, with his mother, Marelle, in a photo taken late in 1909. This and the following sixteen photos, given to the author by Marelle Flynn, have never previously been published.

A note by Marelle Flynn on the back of this photo reads: "Errol aged four, in his tent in the garden—his pirate ship can be seen top right, on the lawn. In the tent he was Robinson Crusoe and his dog was Man Friday."

Note by Marelle Flynn on back of photo: "Errol, aged about 4½, playing in the garden."

*Interesting photo suggest-
ing an influence of his
mother in the theater. Her
comment on back of shot is:
"We went as Pierrettes to
Manly Carnival. Errol was
objecting to wasting his
time being photographed.
He wanted to run—play
with his cousin Ronnie—
my friend Alison is trying
to hold him—we were all
happy & laughing—I am in
the centre."*

*Note by Marelle (continues
from previous shot of the Pierrettes): "And in the next picture—he closed his eyes just to
pay us out—I heard him telling Ronnie—and sure enough
when the snap was developed
we found that he actually had
closed his eyes. I kept it because I thought it was so funny.
(I am at the top.)"*

Note by Marelle: "In this one he is more himself—a sunny little humorist—I am the tallest one at the end. I was then about 21." Mrs. Flynn may have erred on her age. She would have been twenty-three or twenty-four, unless she married Professor Flynn at sixteen or seventeen. Anyway, that's her note above.

Note by Marelle: "Errol minds the baby (his sister Rosemary) about 1921. London."

Note by Marelle: "Errol on a Sydney Beach NSW [New South Wales]. Question. Who owns the umbrella?"

Note by Marelle: "Errol in Hobart about 1924."

Errol at age seventeen or eighteen as a cadet officer in the Australian service at Sydney, on his way to patrol duty in New Guinea. Here began his cane-carrying style.

*Errol, aged about
nineteen, still in New
Guinea with the
police service, along-
side a native.*

*Below: Errol (on the
far left) as a cadet
officer with a band of
New Guineans.*

Photo taken by Errol at Port Moresby, New Guinea, while with the District Officer's service.

Headquartered at Sydney, Errol has time for girls. This note by Marelle on the back of the snapshot: "Errol doing some window courting —Boroval NSW [New South Wales] about 1927. (Mr. Dibbs Residence.)" Errol was for a time engaged to Naomi Dibbs.

In 1930 when Errol was about twenty-one he and three companions set out in a sailboat, the Sirocco, on a trip from Sydney to New Guinea by way of the coastal waters of Australia. Sirocco is the name of a warm Mediterranean wind. This photo shows Errol on board the craft.

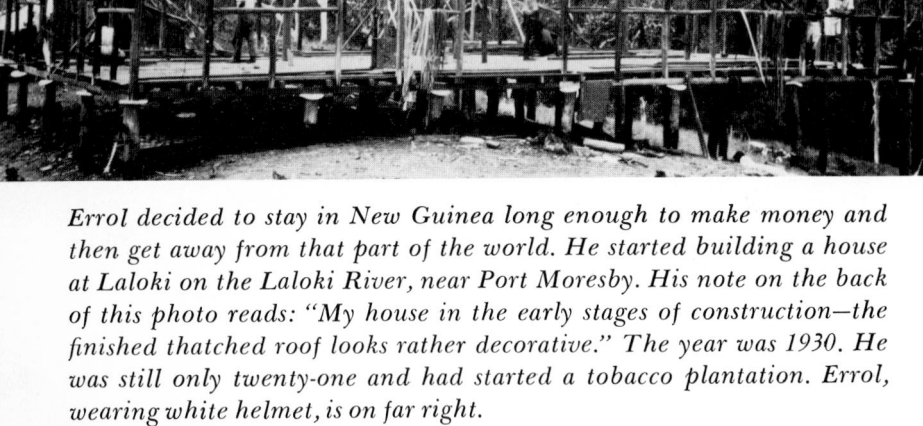

Errol decided to stay in New Guinea long enough to make money and then get away from that part of the world. He started building a house at Laloki on the Laloki River, near Port Moresby. His note on the back of this photo reads: "My house in the early stages of construction—the finished thatched roof looks rather decorative." The year was 1930. He was still only twenty-one and had started a tobacco plantation. Errol, wearing white helmet, is on far right.

Errol's house after construction was finished.

Marelle Flynn and Professor Theodore Flynn upon their arrival in the United States to visit their famous son.

Below: Marelle Flynn and Professor Flynn reaching their hotel after arriving in the United States. They have been trailed by photographers and by public relations people from Warner Brothers.

The sea was very probably the great love of Flynn's life. After his trial, he bought a new boat and called it the Zaca, a Samoan word meaning peace. This is a shot of the craft in the vicinity of Majorca, Spain, where it was moored for years.

Right: Errol on board the Zaca at Majorca. He is in his forties and no longer with Warner Brothers.

Errol Flynn and Earl Conrad on the patio of the Titchfield Hotel, Port Antonio, Jamaica, early in October, 1949. The research on the autobiography is almost done. It is noontime, under a hot sun. The mark of time is there in this very late photo.

often tried, he sighed, but couldn't achieve it there. "Not with anyone," he said, "and I've tried and tried."

Others, those who look for hard ways to do simple things, have asserted this can be done. But Errol said it was impossible—for him at least.

Sad too because he spent so much of his life in, around and underneath water.

Errol, up there in heaven—surely that is where he is (and rather a problem there, I'm sure)—will have no objection to the limning of this detail.

"Don't be astounded, sport. [That Australian idiom. I was always "sport" to him.] The drawing card must be something else: my face and form, my movies, my money, my bout with the world, the front page—but it isn't because the ladies have been circulating any rumors about the length of my good right arm."

"Errol," I said, "speaking as your Boswell I think that controversial item of yours needs to be photographed. Maybe we can get the publisher to put it on the back of the jacket or something—for posterity, you know—just to let them know we're doing an honest book."

He laughed, thinking I was joking, which I was. He said, "When we get back Stateside I promise to have it recorded on film. Perhaps press it into a bit of cement in front of Grauman's."

Yet my blithe and nonserious suggestion of some historical photography bore issue a couple of months later. . . .

Errol was tramping over a Cuban road on the short march with Fidel Castro, helping the radical leader to liberate Cubans from Batista—or at least helping to keep Hollywood in the news. A photographer was alongside, of course.

He stopped at the side of a road to take a pee. There he

stood, hand upon his micturitor pointed at the earth, and the photographer caught that moment in time.

The film wasn't developed until it was delivered to a news syndicate located in the New York Times Building. I chanced to be outside the darkroom waiting to see what the photography would reveal. (I was helping him do a series of articles on the Castro march for King Features.)

Of a sudden out popped an aide exclaiming, "Look here!"

Several of us (writer, photographers and an agent) huddled over a desk looking at the photo of Errol standing there peeing in the Revolution. I decided then and there this shot could not be sent out for publication across the land.

"No mats," I murmured. "But hang onto it."

Foresighted, or is it farsighted, photographers printed up a number of copies of this extraordinary eight by ten photo: Errol in suitclothes, looking lean, a bit harassed, not too revolutionary, but intent upon the good earth. It has been circulating about in the photographic underground for the past sixteen or seventeen years.

The last time I heard of its existence was in San Francisco, where a local photographer invited me to the office of *Rolling Stone,* for he said he knew of a unique picture of Flynn taken in Cuba.

"I've seen it," I told him. "I was there almost at its birth, and though it's a shot of the most famous cutlass of the twentieth century, I don't need to see it again. I have seen the original."

I may have sounded a bit like Cortes when with eagle eyes/he stared at the Pacific/with a wild surmise/silent upon a peak in Darien.

Errol would like that; he loved Keats and all poetry.

So there was Errol, standing amid the Revolution, letting it all hang out long before the expression was coined. He was at the side of a ditch or half into it, and the background was semijungle, bush, stalk and sky: and Flynn was up front in his own kind of "Salud."

For the first couple of weeks I was with him something secretive had been going on. Dhondi would say, "Errol wants to take a nap. Come back later," and I would leave. Or Errol would say, "Why don't you go for a swim, Earl. I'll tidy up." I noticed that these casual intermissions or gentle dismissals always occurred when a ramshackle car drove up to the hotel, two people got out, a man and a woman, and went up to Errol's quarters. I might spot them from the swimming pool, or the hotel garden or the bar. They would be upstairs with him half an hour or so, and as silently, mysteriously, come out of the lobby, get into their car and make off. Sometimes I got a call after these visits. Dhondi might yell out from their window, "Errol wants to work." I would swiftly locate the court reporter, who might be typing in his quarters. I noticed that at such times Errol spoke with a remarkable calm and flow and ease.

It took me two or three weeks to learn he was on heavy drugs. Later I would learn it was mainly morphine, and that he needed an injection about every three days. The doctor motored across the island from Kingston, sixty miles away.

One night Errol had withdrawal symptoms. He was writhing in bed in terrible agony. I saw him twisting, turning, grappling with his stomach, placing his hands on his thighs and the calves of his legs for relief from whatever was straining at his nerves or his muscles. He was also making utterances of great pain.

I had never seen him this way before and would never see
him quite that way again.

It was terrible to behold.

Calls went out to the local doctors. They wouldn't budge.
There were only two or three in the place, a town of ten or
twelve thousand people. Errol was an old client of theirs
from years back and they were weary of feeding him drugs,
of ministering to his temper, his tantrums, his imperious-
ness.

The Kingston physician was finally called. At one in the
morning he and the woman arrived.

Nobody was allowed in the room while the physician took
care of Errol. I was outside with Dhondi.

When the doctor came out he didn't say anything to us.

He had driven sixty miles across the island, and now he
was driving back to Kingston. The moon lighted the road.
Palm silhouettes were everywhere. Auto lights illuminated
the scrub, the cutlass-shaped stalks of grass.

In his room Errol was stretched out half asleep, quieted.
He would get through the night.

For reasons that Errol said he never understood, small
men wanted to fight him. In a bar some small man, with a
few drinks in him, might get nasty, insult him, call him a
fraud, put up his hands and say, "Let's see you fight, you
yellow this or that."

Errol said he almost never put up his dukes at these
sessions, but was always poised inwardly to do so, and
nervously ready to counterattack in the flick of an instant
if he had to. One swat from him would likely lay the intrepid
challenger low.

Rather mystically he said, "What do I excite in some

people, especially small men?" Were they jealous of his
size, name, reputation? Did they get a kind of identification
out of hoping to say, "I fought Flynn"? He estimated he
had been in a dozen or more of these mindless engage-
ments. Some had been bitter five-minute fights.

One evening something like that seemed afoot, except
that the challenger was as big as Flynn, younger, looking
physical and formidable. They were having a noisy wrangle
on a piazza of the Titchfield, while the adjoining ballroom
was alight with dancers, music, fun.

Cruise ships from the States made Port Antonio one of
their overnight stops. The ballroom of the Titchfield was
then used for an evening of entertainment, dancing, vaude-
ville and the like—and that was happening this evening.

At ten o'clock when the entertainment and the gay mood
reached its height Errol got the idea that it might be nice
if Dhondi had a moment up in front of the orchestra to sing,
dance a few steps and entertain. She was a lively entertainer, with a repertoire of popular songs she belted out sweetly.

Errol had arranged for her to go on for about five minutes. But the cruise master in charge of entertainment for
the ship—this big fellow—stepped in to oppose the idea.
The girl was not with the band; outsiders did not participate in the entertainment; he was in charge of it and would
run the ballroom events and the program.

Word went back to Errol that Dhondi would not be allowed to do her bit. Errol, asking to know who was respon-
sible for the decision, was suddenly in this hot contention,
off to the side with this large chap, wanting to know what
crime would be committed if the young girl sang a song or
two.

I chanced to be not far away when I heard the rising

voices and looked in that direction. Errol beckoned me to
come over while he stood face to face with the cruise master.

I walked to their side, stood a few feet away and heard
the loud talk, the threats emanating from both. You won't!
I will! You can't! I can! She can! She will! We'll see! We
certainly will see! Like hell you will! You stay out of this!
I'm running this show! Maybe you are, maybe not!

I was catching all of this rapid fire. Others gathered
around. Errol's face and neck were red. So were the other
guy's.

It would have been a terrible brawl. It would have undone the evening's entertainment, upset the hotel manage-
ment, the people on the cruise, Dhondi and all the rest of
us.

It was at the moment when I thought fists were about to
fly that, as suddenly as it all erupted, it died down. Each
turned simultaneously and moved off.

It was as if each knew something terrible would happen
if the blows began to fall.

I never could figure out what separated them, what
ended the thing. Had the cruise master noticed the way
Errol beckoned me over and the way I stood by, witness
fashion? Had that been a factor? Had Errol decided to
withdraw?

It was like two roosters who, instead of attacking, suddenly back off.

I was glad it was an incipient brawl that never developed.

Neither he nor I ever mentioned the incident except
for one poignant remark he made the next day. "All I
wanted was for Small Companion to have a moment in
the sun."

•   •   •

Each day I questioned him, poked at his memory. At these sessions he would be voluble from the first minute through to the time when he would murmur, "Guess we've had it."

Then we would go through diverse paces the rest of the day: a swim, drinks at the bar, meals, or I'd be standing aloof as he wrangled with Dhondi. I was privy to his entire mode of living, what he had told the Jamaica *Gleaner* was "a fair day in the tropics."

He knew his story emerged from him in a raw, disjointed way, so he asked from time to time, "How are you going to put all this together?"

"Leave that to me, Errol," I answered.

The new secretary at the Titchfield desk was about twenty-three, a light-complected Jamaica girl with Anglo features. She had lovely eyes, with an Oriental cast: slits of eyes that revealed no more when she smiled than when she was in repose, but always a gleam in those slits of eyes. A most peculiarly attractive female. She was lean and rapid in her motions and seemed to be almost without breasts. No matter, there was nothing more feminine than she in all Port Antonio. Mostly I remember her voice, with a gentle music to it, and a lilt of the Jamaican idiom.

Errol, as soon as he set eyes upon her on the day of her arrival, remarked to me, "I haven't seen her before. She's new."

She was solicitous of all the details that might concern Errol, and ever so frequently she gave him that subtly Oriental smile with the unmoving eyes that gleamed.

I saw few females who unsettled or disturbed or awakened him in any special way, but did note the magnetism that passed between them. He has a problem, I said to myself; it is Dhondi. He must have been saying about the same thing to himself. I heard Dhondi say to him, "You stay away from her." The attraction between the two was so noticeable that the birds of paradise in the banana trees in the side yard of the Titchfield cackled their interest—and possibly hope.

The time arrived, the night arrived, the hour arrived, the emotions were fully rounded. Dhondi had run off in a spate of anger, and he was left alone to pay court to the little lady of the reception desk.

He disappeared early in the evening with her into one of the rooms of the hotel, not his own suite but a remote place in a rear portion of the Titchfield.

I didn't see him again until the next morning at about nine o'clock.

Then I saw both at the breakfast table on the Titchfield porch. There was an illumination about them.

After she left—she had to get back to work at the hotel desk—I ventured, "How was it?"

"It was like being lashed between two tugboats going down a white river full throttle." (A white river is a foamy, swiftly flowing, heavily currented, rocky waterway.)

"Really?"

He didn't stop there. "It was like hanging onto a rope behind six motorboats, a strand from each craft tied to the strand I hung onto, and being hauled at a hundred miles an hour through a lake full of chism."

I knew that when he drew on imagery of the sea, the ocean, the waterways of the world, he was really inspired. I figured next he would be about a thousand feet below water in some other metaphor—and I was right.

He stopped eating his breakfast. He never ate much anyway. Usually he picked up a couple of crumbs of scrambled

eggs in his fingers, popped them into his mouth like pea-
nuts, and drank his coffee or vodka.

Now he came on as the actor. He had no words left to
describe what happened. There was a moment's halt in his
talk, a reflective glint in his eye.

"I was grateful," he murmured. A halt. "To repay her,"
he said . . . another halt . . . he stared at me as if to say,
"Watch this . . ." then, "I have not often been this kind to
ladies. . . ."

The far-off look went a little further. . . .

Suddenly he tilted his head up a bit and started making
fishlike motions with his mouth and jaw, opening and shut-
ting his lips in a staccato manner.

"They're all sisters under the skin," he said, recollecting
his amours.

I asked what he meant.

He said he was thinking of a famous English lady, a titled
lady. He had met her at a moment in his career when his
triumphs were at the highest; after he had made *The Adventures of Robin Hood,* and the world of high Washington was
open to him; so was the English court. This happened in
Britain. . . .

He had been given royal treatment at the British court,
hailed as a Briton by ancestry, celebrated as a recent stu-
dent of the Northampton Repertory, and then, in the
United States, he had become a huge success and a credit
to the English land. He was introduced around, and among
those he met was this stylish, reserved and ladylike Duchess.

"Me meeting a real Duchess," he said to himself at the
time.

"And she was behaving like a Duchess." There had been

tea, crumpets, servants, elegant discussion, references to the great and the near great of Great Britain.

"I was on my mettle," Errol said, "no fancy overtures toward this one. Treat her like a lady."

He went on, "I bowed and scuffed and put on airs and held my teacup as daintily as she did."

Then, said Errol, she suddenly murmured, "Errol, my dear, we are alone. The Duke has gone to Kensington. He'll be away a fortnight. I have been (pronounced bean, to Americans) veddy much by myself. I am so delighted you are here tonight."

Errol said his little finger on the teacup wavered and his thumb straightened perceptibly.

She was leaning forward in a beautifully upholstered chair opposite his beautifully upholstered chair.

"At sea," said Errol, "I was trained never to question a flag of distress. At sea I hoisted sails and sped swiftly to whomever needed me—as seamen have sped to my help. I sped to hers."

He placed the cup of tea on the table to his right and rose like a guard at Buckingham Palace, and in one majestic sweep put his arms around her "and I grabbed her good.

"She started dragging me, as if I were a Bengali rebel, to her gallows in an adjoining room. I let myself be dragged and managed to get my fingers into the back of her dress at the neck, where I could tear it off with the most ease. It looked like an expensive dress, too.

"In a moment we were there on the Duke's own bed.

"All that I remember the great lady saying before the bout began was exactly what Rosie O'Grady must have said in similar circumstances:

" 'Oh Ehrelll, Oh Ehrelll, fook me! Fook me!' "

So much for great ladies.

At the risk of wrecking the foregoing I venture this:

His reaction of astonishment might have harked back to his idealistic days in New Guinea when he dreamed of going up in British politics and perhaps even reaching the Parliament, where indubitably he would meet "great ladies." Maybe he thought they were so great that they were above and beyond any such crass biological concerns.

Here was his life—or part of it—unfolding before me by the hour, running from wildness to errancy to absurdity to blatant tragedy, then back to farce.

Still I never had the feeling anything wrong or porny or improper was going on. Rather, there was a barnyard simplicity about it. My own rearing had been rather formal, a heavy tinge of monogamy in my background and a conviction I ought properly to be living that way myself, difficult as it often is when a beautiful woman goes by. Most of the time I couldn't see where Errol was hurting anyone by being his sexual self. The women seemed satisfied, especially those he paid with cash.

But don't get me wrong: he had a touch of macho in him and could get an extra sexual kick out of a bit of cruelty now and then, which to his thinking was fun.

When Errol talked about his light amours and lapsed into his "fatuous" approach to sex (fatuous was his favorite word to describe his lifestyle), he was on his own and I had less need to ask questions.

But he really sprang alive when we moved into philosophy, the so-called fundamentals, the reputed verities of the act of living. Then and there I touched his central chords; then he was enlivened, mystified and most involved. Life, death, war, peace, politics, religion, creativity: being of use, doing something useful, these were his central ingredients.

He was into life itself, its swift passing, his conviction that the turned-up earth ended it all. He was concerned whether he had left creative impact. He worried that he had never resolved his drive to write something memorable. I assured him his book would be that: that he had *authored his own unique life* whereas many authors have merely authored *books.*

I said, "The two can't be compared. A billion people can tell some kind of story. Only a few can tell the story of an age because they have been in on part of that age."

He was happy to hear that, so, when we would finish talking about one of his female bouts, or a movie, or a brawl in public with someone, I brought the questioning back to Hegel, Marx, Aristotle, Socrates, Seneca, Euripedes, the Greeks, the Romans, the Jews. Then he was knowledgeable in a way a man is knowledgeable who studies by hurricane lamp: self-education.

I saw on him the mark of his scientist father.

When we went into that realm, the fun and cynicism left his features. A new, a serious animation came over him, for he wanted more than all else to talk about his battle with the "verities."

Thirty years earlier, on August 17, 1930, he had written to his father from Cooktown while on board his sailboat, the *Sirocco,* ending his letter:

As soon as I've got a credit balance of several hundred I'm going to take myself to Cambridge to study History & Literature —I've been coming to the conclusion for a long time that the most vital thing in Life is to be able to understand it.

All my love and respect Dad
from Errol

But after three decades and all that he had experienced he came into a cynical doubt. He decided the quest had led him to nothing. For, when he looked at this letter in the galleys of *Wicked Ways*, he changed the last sentence to read:

I've been coming to the conclusion for a long time that the most vital thing in Life is to be able to understand it. God, what profundity, eh?

All my love and respect Dad
from Errol

Thirty years later he pooh-poohed his search as a stupid quest, mocked it, laughed at his early idealism. And he struck off his disillusion with that last cryptic phrase, "God, what profundity, eh?"

Probably no man ever understood less of life after trying to understand it than he. He had set out to find understanding by experiencing life sensorily or sensually or sexually or sensationally: all of these. He must put the world to the test of his senses, perhaps thinking this was life.

Now he had done this and had succeeded perhaps beyond even his drives. He had international fame, had made a fortune, had women at his feet and his crotch, men jealous of his attainments: he was at heights, he had leaped from one height to another. In the great art of the day, the cinema, he had emerged as one of the giants. Some of his performances endured in the annals of film literature.

True, some other things had not been achieved. Instead of the great career in Literature and at the Bar, ambitions he had earlier expressed to his father, there had been his infamous and disillusioning period in court on the allegation of rape: not one, but two young ladies in one false charge. Some twists, some turns, some disappointments. The arms of women alone had provided him with no great answer. Alcohol turned in no philosophic conclusions. Morphine had given him no perceptions about why, when, whither. Still, beneath the public clown, beneath the roustabout of the saloons, the seas and the international resorts, there was still a thoughtful lad trying to penetrate the world's riddles.

In his diary this agnostic, this fellow who hated the church, who always referred derogatorily to his mother as "Christ-bitten," this strange being who, alone in the jungles often had nothing to read but labels on cans . . . and the Bible . . . seemed to turn back to God, as an answer, if only one could touch, reach, find, feel, believe in God.

Read this written in Rome or Naples either in 1952 or 1953. The dating seems unclear, but he says he is in his early forties at the time. It is entered in his diary somewhat like a complete essay, and it is one of the few topics to which he gives a title:

FAITH?

Some say that we shall never know God's purpose, that there is no God nor any purpose, that we humans are like the ants crushed under a boy's foot for the fun of it.

But then there are those who will tell you with firm conviction that never a flea jumped from a dog's back that God didn't know of.

What is Faith? And why are you born with or without it? For certainly from what I have observed in this life, Faith is not a thing you develop. On the contrary, if I have developed anything definite it is a dull smouldering anger at the abysmal mystery of my presence on this earth, with not the least clue to any reason for it; a mystery that probably not even death will solve for me. Why am I alive?

What, then, is Faith? In what? Today, in my early forties I find myself in a state of tortured confusion where my every past action or experience, my daily movements are measured and appraised by one who does not seem to be myself; an alter ego who stands by with detached and contemptuous mien, sneering at the bumbling efforts of a human in search of a soul; a human daily more wrought upon and bewildered by the external questions: "Whence do I come? What am I? Whither do I go?" ??? [The question marks are inscribed in his diary in the squarish form that characterized the question mark he always wore on his suit.]

Swept by doubt, desperately seeking just one little sign from Heaven—the sign that those of Faith do not demand, I am carried along like duckweed down a Chinese river, feeling yet always denying the existence of a benign Deity, knowing so goddamn well in my heart that I have reached the supreme goal of egoistic existence. For what?

Faith. Why does it elude me? Why cannot I find peace of mind like those I envy? Those who have listened and heard & felt, and having done so, contritely let fall all other barriers and started to believe wholeheartedly in God?

Why am I even unable to begin by renouncing the material things, the transitory & ephemeral? Why, knowing—and knowing, strangely, with humility—my faults, my myriad imperfections, do I go on with outward complacency, yet with growing inward desolation? Why must my mind remain factual, materialist whilst within me I stifle my cry for help and will not yield an iota to the stumbling craving in my soul? Will this rebellion against God never end?

Quos deus vult perdere, prius dementat. [Whom the gods wish to destroy, they first make mad.] Perhaps this is what is happening to me—or maybe I can seek solace in the thought I am only going through a sort of male menopause.

So this life is only a preparation for a hereafter? This is still an illogical premise to explain the period of human history in which I have lived. The graveyards at Anzio and ten million of the world's finest men swallowed up, sacrificed upon the most incomprehensible of all mankind's bizarre altars—man's inhumanity to man, war.

Twice, three times that number could probably be accounted for, if Russia and China were included. Was it the Sublime purpose to abbreviate for these millions of souls the preparation for the hereafter in anguish and torture? And now we prepare for the unspeakable horrors of yet another war, with weapons which may well portend mankind's final self destruction.

So Faith is a word the meaning of which eludes me. I mean Faith in the concept of a benign all-seeing God. God, in the sense of a creator, yes. God in the sense of a Supreme Being I can believe in. But a God who believes in me, a God who is aware of my soul's existence, who after death will clear up the great mystery of my reason for life in this world, in this God I have no faith, nor can I begin to seek it with a full heart.

Today I see a strange world, more bewildering and paradoxical than anything I have read in history, even the birth of Christianity —one half of mankind grimly devoted to the task of stamping out the idea of God & Religion; the other half apathetic to both. Supine and hypocritical, the professed believers in a Christian God today give lip-service in the various totem-houses, listening in private to their priests denounce the other Christian sects with hatred & malice. In the light of the Church's sordid history, its stubborn refusal to keep pace with modern thought, its failure to satisfy the religious needs of today perhaps this apathy is understandable.

The world's need for Faith is desperate, more desperate than my own, for I am only one lost individual in a tortured universe, a world weary, shocked and shattered. No philosophy, no political fanatical dogma can stand against a true belief in God.

Faith—I wish I had it.

That is quite a statement, strange and sad. Perhaps Errol Flynn was in that meditation Everyman.

Who that read of Flynn in the papers, his latest quip in a nightclub, his latest blonde, his latest caper with the law, his latest trip on the *Zaca* down through the South Seas, could think that beneath his zesty living, behind his façade of the public brawler of the cinema world, lay this prober still thinking the thoughts of his New Guinea days, still wondering what life was all about, what he and others meant, what anything meant, tormented by quest. *Quest.* A modern Ulysses, living out the paradoxes of modern times in his daily experiences while others only read of the paradoxes on the front page. Flynn on a cross of his own all through World War II (the rape case that amused the multitude while the Nazis were driving East), Flynn in the 1950s with his *Zaca* moored outside Franco's Spain (the same Spain toward which he headed full of sympathy for the Loyalists in 1938), Flynn who was psychologically a British imperialist but destined to live the early part of his life with Stone Age people, Flynn tossed between the power of Great Britain and the Woolamaloo gang dregs of Sydney, Australia.

As the weeks went by I continued to learn about the young Flynn, still on his way across the seven seas to get to England, a driving, forceful figure about to set the world on its tail.

On board the Manila-bound ship Errol struck up with a giant of a man, Dr. Gerrit Koets. He was a Hollander, a scientist and medical man who was in New Guinea on a foundation grant to seek a solution to hookworm, a major malaise of that part of the world. Koets had been all over the world. He and Flynn were much alike, Errol said: each was interested in women, money, knowledge and endless daily adventure and change.

With time—during the next eight months as they romped together across the seven seas until Errol reached England, visiting whorehouses, being in wrangles almost everywhere, passing from one raucous wild time to another and barely living through it all—Errol took on some of the lifestyle of the other. They became fast friends, a friendship that was to resume when Errol became famous in Hollywood.

In the Philippines Errol and Koets became interested in cockfighting. Koets taught Errol how to use snake venom on a rooster in order to win a bet on which bird would win. There was warfare with police, with Filipinos gypped of their bets; finally a mad race to board the *Empress of Asia* bound for Hong Kong. Their adventures went on like that for months. They bet on ponies in China; they got to Macao, a gambling center fit for rovers like Errol and Koets to ply their nefarious gambits; then a Chinese beauty named Ting Ling who introduced Errol to opium, to gambling dens, to the freakish sights of wanton Macao. It turned out Ting Ling was as much a hooker as Errol was; she made off with several thousand of his dollars.

Broke in Hong Kong, he and Koets stood on a pier wondering what to do, how to live. So they joined the Royal Hong Kong Volunteers, an army of English and Chinese alliance against a threatened Japanese invasion. But their job was to dig snow for weeks. It didn't appeal to them. They deserted, faked passports, hopped onto a packet that took them to a boat carrying them to Ceylon, India. Errol had the gall to write to his father that he was on "a voyage of discovery." Marelle Flynn took that seriously. In a letter she wrote to me after Errol's death she used that expression, "voyage of discovery," as if her son was an "intrepid explorer."

So far they had been lucky, but at a place called Pondichery, Errol, hesitating to tip a rickshaw driver properly, found himself in a bitter quarrel, and in a stroke the agile Indian cut Errol's belly open from scrotum to navel. Then, hospitalization, sixteen stitches, no payment to the hospital, escape from Pondichery. Calcutta, Africa, French Somaliland, brawls; the Red Sea, Ethiopia, the Suez Canal, Marrakech in French Morocco, months of wandering, but ever getting closer to the "mother land." At Marseilles, Errol and Koets parted company. Koets headed back to continental Europe, Errol to London. Errol felt a great debt to Koets for his lifestyle, outlook and philosophy. He claimed Koets showed him the importance of the complete irrelevance of existence, the unimportance of being earnest, the need to laugh at the worst disasters. Errol was to have many of these disasters in the years to come, and one wonders whether he really laughed at them.

He arrived in London with the usual difficulties—money troubles, inability to pay hotel costs, wires back and forth between himself and his father now at Heidelberg University. Errol made a decisive turn in his career thinking. He bluffed his way into the Northampton Repertory Theater, and there he stayed a year and a half doing yeoman performances: butlers, detectives, burglars, gentlemen, even playing the part of an old maid. It was great training for him, and the girls were good. Over and over he narrowly escaped marriage, always running away from women as he had from his mother. He played Shakespearean roles, Bulldog Drummond, and even wrote a play called *Cold Rice*. In fact, all of his days thereafter he tried to combine his acting with his literary inclination.

Somewhere in this period he hit upon the word "fatuous." He felt that his own days were spent in much foolish living, and yet he felt that this was the way to live. Foolishness and fun, whiling the time away at pleasure. These were verities to him and they would be all the days of his life.

He made it to the Stratford-on-Avon Festival. This was at the West End, a point of arrival for any actor. Irving Asher, a Hollywood scout, involved Errol in a motion picture part in a film called *Murder at Monte Carlo*. It was a cops-and-robbers item that Jack Warner soon saw, and Errol was called to Hollywood. But the significant incident was that on his way to New York, aboard *The Paris*, he met the famed actress Lili Damita.

Of a sudden he was launched in films; at the outset secondary roles in *The Case of the Curious Bride* and *Don't Bet on Blondes*. But his wife was the famed Damita, then an arrived actress. Her friends were the noted directors and agents of cinemaland, and Errol, through her, made connections. When the actor Robert Donat passed up the role of *Captain Blood* and Errol landed it, a new chapter in the life of Hollywood films began. Overnight Errol became the swashbuckling successor of Douglas Fairbanks. Fan mail began—and never ended. But troubles with Lili Damita also began. Women were after him, and Errol couldn't be snared and captained by any one woman.

Successful films came on rapidly thereafter for five or six years: *The Charge of the Light Brigade, Green Light, The Prince and the Pauper, Another Dawn, The Perfect Specimen*. And then a film that lighted up the whole entertainment world, *Robin Hood*—Errol in his classic role, a role very like the character of Errol himself. Nobody was making more money for Warner Brothers now than Errol. With him, paired in several of these films, was the beautiful young actress Olivia deHavilland.

The screen magazines were filled with his flair, the gossip

of his private life, hints of his drinking and flamboyance. He was thirty-one now and was in one box office attraction after another: *The Dawn Patrol, The Sisters, Four's a Crowd,* the lead man for Bette Davis in *The Private Lives of Elizabeth and Essex. The Sea Hawk* made in that year was one of his finest performances.

In 1941 he and Damita were finished. Later his settlement with her called for him to pay fifteen hundred dollars a month for so long as she remained unmarried—and Lili Damita never did remarry until after Errol's death.

The great pressures of movie- and money-making were now a strain. He seemed always to be in a wrangle with Jack Warner over salary and vehicles. He badly needed escape, and at that point his old friend Gerrit Koets reached Hollywood. That was the signal for a new spate of off-camera adventures. He and Koets beat it to New York where he got another dose of the "Pearl of Great Price"; then they went off to Spain. A good war was on, and Errol and Koets always welcomed such sports.

Surviving that war on the Loyalist side—and a few shots fired at him—Errol returned to this country and to the wars of Hollywood.

By now—1940 and 1941—the whole world was at war. Errol's starring friends were in the armed services, but Errol was 4-F on two counts: recurrent malaria and a touch of tuberculosis. He tried to enter each service but was rejected. His buddies, actors like David Niven and Clark Gable, were in the service. Errol had no great fear of wars: he had been to Spain; he had done a short shift of ditch digging with the Hong Kong Volunteers; New Guinea was a form of war; and now he, the great warrior of English mythology, he of Sherwood Forest and "service" as Captain Blood, was out of it. They only wanted to use him as an entertainer of the troops. What a role!

During this time there was nothing left for him to do but pursue his various careers: women, films, big money.

No one has yet told the story, or ferreted out the truth, why the Los Angeles authorities moved on Errol in late 1942 to accuse him of statutory rape for an incident that allegedly occurred two years earlier. The story, if and when it does get told (and in Hollywood eventually everything is revealed), will have to do with the rivalry at that time between Los Angeles officialdom and the power of the motion picture industry.

To the whole world Los Angeles was Hollywood, films, famous celebrities, entertainment, fun, the lighter more desirable side of life. Upcoming lawyers and politicians in the big city felt upstaged and put down by the aura that surrounded the movie biggies, the producers, the actors and the big money in that realm. There was a long history of payoffs by the Hollywood moguls to the piddling politicians for hushing up scandals, protecting actors and actresses.

It all closed in on Errol one night when two lawmen stopped off at his Mulholland House and served a paper on him, told him they had a charge of statutory rape preferred against him by a young lady then in Juvenile Hall. Her case was weak, but the District Attorney's office moved to bring in another young lady, and of a sudden Errol had four charges against him. Still, in a few days a grand jury threw out the charges. According to Errol, the jury "saw something that stank." Errol thought he had escaped the situation, but shortly afterward the District Attorney's office, in a cantankerous frame of mind, with some big stake behind its moves, came down again on Errol.

On the same night that Errol thought he was free of the problem, he received a phone call in which someone calling himself Joe demanded that Errol go to Jack Warner, get ten thousand bucks and pay off at a certain street corner directly, or on Wednesday the world would tumble in on Flynn.

Errol ignored the call, and on Wednesday the District Attorney's office revived the charges, overrode the grand jury and reopened Errol's case. For five months the headlines of newspapers all over the country—even all over the world—featured Errol's troubles. The incident provided some relief from the horrors of the then raging World War II. Finally, after Jerry Geisler defended the actor in court, Errol was acquitted.

To Errol's thinking, as to most people, correctly, rape is a forcible act against a woman's will. If there was one fellow in the world who never needed to rape a woman it was Errol Flynn, for women fell all over him and threw themselves at him.

Now that he was freed he felt in total disgrace, felt his career was ruined. Instead of being a wartime hero he was an international scapegoat.

He began to seek ways of killing himself. But he was unable to shoot himself in the head with the pistol he aimed at his temple for three hours at one time, debating with himself about his family responsibilities, thinking of his parents, his career, the pileup of his life. Instead he chose drink, drugs (he had already had this experience) and living it up. He would be the guy they said he was, let it all hang out and go to hell! With this decision or shift in soul and psychology there came to be the public Errol Flynn that the world remembers: the prankster, wild man of the mattress. The slogan "In like Flynn" rose like smoke from the trial and ran laughingly around the globe. Errol grinned back at the world and decided to live out his days as a fun-sex figure. A decision like that is somewhat like a funeral epitaph over one's own soul.

Although after his rape case Errol was still making $200,000 a picture, he was as unhappy and disjointed a rich man as fortune ever devised. He kept thinking of the altered course of his life. Unable to kill himself, he returned to his first great love, the sea. He bought an ex-Navy ship, named it the *Zaca,* a Samoan term for peace, spent $50,000 fixing it up, placed the symbol of a crowing rooster on the house flag he flew, and decided to sail the seas as much as possible for the rest of his days.

He planned a cruise with his father to the Galápagos islands, six hundred miles west of Ecuador in the Pacific. It was to be a sentimental journey to echo Darwin's voyage of the *Beagle.* A party of Hollywood celebrities was organized to go along, but somehow the trip fell apart. As they reached La Jolla, members of the party dropped out and returned to Hollywood. At Acapulco his father also dropped out and returned to Los Angeles.

Errol and his crew went on alone, visited the Cocos Islands, passed through the Panama Canal and entered the waters of the Caribbean. Errol was happy on board, doing the night watch, watching the skies, breathing the salt spray and directing the course of the ship when another development altered his remaining days. A hurricane arrived and swept the yacht for four days along its edge. No one knew where they were. On the fourth day, moving along a coastal

region neither he nor any of his crew could identify, fearing
the craft would go aground, someone spotted a port a few
miles away. The ship moved toward it and entered a sunny
harbor. What continent? Errol wondered. As the ship slid
into port people gathered on shore to see the strange sight,
a ghostly slow-moving ship. As Errol stepped onto the
wharf he was recognized and told that this was Kingston,
Jamaica.

In the days that followed Errol fell in love with the island
of Jamaica. It reminded him of his years in New Guinea
waters: black people, jungle, palm trees, birds of paradise,
frangipani, poinsetta, warmth.

At the age of thirty-seven, after a lifetime of wandering,
he had found an island for home and rest.

From time to time we went hunting the big snook on the
Rio Grande. A beautiful river if God ever made one, it ran
from Port Antonio inland through Jamaica jungle. Errol
said that in stormy seasons the river was ferocious, flying
over the banks, sopping up the jungle all about, roaring
and whirling.

Now the waters were low.

Native Jamaicans, black, muscular, excelling in and
around the water, poled the bamboo raft down the river.

Throughout these gliding, half-sensuous trips, with bird
calls providing us with music, Errol sipped a drink. He
carried with him, on the raft, an attaché case on which were
the words "Flynn Enterprises." Inside were vodka, bottles
of tonic, glasses.

He would dive below, in one of the baylets of the river.
"I'll bring him up barehanded," he vowed.

I dearly wanted to see him catch the big snook.

More likely I would see him kill himself in one of his almost daily encounters with the deep sea.

I sat in a rowboat far out in the Navy Island channel, in Caribbean waters, waiting for him to surface.

He had been tumbling about in the boat for some time, adjusting his headgear and unscrambling a spear. Then he had carefully gone over the side of the boat and descended out of sight.

I hoped the oxygen tank was in good shape. A narrow tube of compressed air going from the tank down to his headgear was all that was between him and life or death.

I had no idea what deep-sea diving was. He seemed at home with the sport. He had told me of a dozen narrow escapes. It seemed as though this was what he wanted, the narrow escape, the risk, the danger, punching death in the face—but surfacing once more.

He was down there five minutes, eight minutes, ten minutes. I didn't see the hose over the side of the boat move anymore. He must be walking on the bottom.

I looked around: the sun shone, sky blue, in the distance the palm-covered shores of the island.

I became restive. What could I do? Was he gone forever?

Nobody was around but myself sitting in that boat.

Then, of a sudden, he surfaced. He swam a few feet to the boat. I reached to help him get inside. He rather fell into the bottom of the boat, removed his headgear. He breathed heavily a minute or so, didn't speak.

"I was worried," I said.

"No need for you to worry," he said.

"Why not?"

"If I had gotten into any trouble down there all you would have been able to do is point to the spot"—he pointed ten yards away—" and tell them, 'He went down there. That's the last I saw of him.' "

I realized I was exactly that helpless: no way I could get him up. For all practical purposes he had gone below entirely on his own, far from land, deep down, just as if I hadn't been there.

Rowing back to shore he described the world down below: big fish swimming close by, thrusting his spear at a fish, the shape of rocks and weeds, shafts of sunlight streaming down through the water.

He moved his eyes sharply from left to right—far to the left, far to the right, back and forth several times. "You have to be alert, like that, you have to watch left and right, above and below, for anything, everything. That alertness means you are more alive than ever."

His eyes swung left and right again to show awareness, tension, his brain at work, his senses alive. He liked to have that kind of exhilaration. He liked to be that much alive—even if the next instant he would be choking to death.

That was what he meant by his "genius for living." Living at the edge of life or death from instant to instant: getting that high intensity each minute as if it were the last. A stinging thrill perennially all the days of his life.

I realized he lived that way much of the time. Nearly every day he chose one or two challenging moments like that or the day was lost.

When he had survived the test, his face and body glowed, there was an excitement, a brightness in his features, over his skin, as if his soul cried: I did it again! I did it again!

But for me there was a queasiness, an unease in being alongside him literally day and evening. Because I was aware I was with a man who was already feeling death and "living" with it.

That is a terrible working experience. It is similar to knowing a loved one is suffering an incurable disease and will pass on in days or weeks or months and we see and feel an aura of the inevitable around the person.

There was no evident disease about Errol to give that impression. Externally at least he was almost as physical as ever: he arose each day, put in that intense living experience, moved and had to be moving, did and had to be doing. Why then the aura of death?

I told him I thought he needlessly risked his life in his deep-sea diving. Why did he do it?

That throaty laugh.

Sometimes dejection descended upon him suddenly. His shoulders slumped, his face went cold; his eyes looked about forlornly or seemed devoid. Then he invariably stood up, if he were sitting, and moved back to his room. These moods might occur when he was with a group of people, at a party, or conversing at a table, and he would appear to be quite sober. It came over him like a cloud. Not long after that he would need a fix and I would see the Kingston doctor and the woman in their rattly car come tearing into the hotel yard.

These seizures or descents always upset me. There was nothing I or anyone else could do about them but watch him walk out. Morphine was the only remedy, and how much of a remedy that was in actuality I don't know.

When that down-low mood hit him he became at once the opposite of all that he was when he was funny or nonsensical. He became grim, mortal, forbidding. When he walked away in that frame of mind it was like a madman willingly entering his own straitjacket.

He had been close to death only a few years earlier.

In the mid-1950s when he was in Spain and Majorca, he took sick with a liver ailment, jaundice, and he entered a Swiss hospital.

He wrote in his diary an account of the experience. He described the reaction of a Thomas Mann character who was tormented by the imminence of approaching death. This character had read something about death being some sort of All-One Theory, nothing final about it, and afterward the character, in Thomas Mann's words, "felt that his whole being had been unaccountably expanded and there clung to his senses a profound intoxication, a strange, sweet vague allurement. He was no longer prevented from grasping eternity."

Errol, who had been that close to finality during the jaundice crisis, recorded:

A gay whimsical fellow full of good cheer told me my liver had now stopped functioning and that atrophy had begun. I don't think I even lifted my eyebrows. Far from stunned, I felt only a mild resentment at my liver, an ingrate if I ever heard of one, undeserving of the good treatment I had always meted (never more than a bottle a day). The young and cheery Swiss had a bedside manner perfectly calculated to soothe the fevered brow of those about to kick off. Cheerful, bright, with a nice grin.

"I see," I said, after he had drawn a clever diagram of my liver that looked surprisingly like the shape of Mexico. "Well, what happens if it doesn't start functioning again soon?"

"You die," he shouted cheerfully. Grinning still cheerfully he passed his hand across his head diagonally from left temple to right, smoothing down long imaginary remnants of reddish blond hair that might once have flourished there.

"Look again at my diagram—how is it possible for you to live?" the Swiss went on. "Not tomorrow, perhaps. Maybe. But certainly day after tomorrow. First, if you will not die your fever must go down. It is bad, your fever, yes. You are worried about something?"

"No, no," I answered. "No, not really." I could have injected a nice sardonic note in here adding something like, "I was just wondering if you have any idea what time exactly I can expect to kick off day after tomorrow?" but the truth of it was I wasn't worried enough, not even stunned.

It was only after the door had closed on that sunny presence, staying abed awhile, then I crawled out and with the firm stride of a man using two wilted asparagus tips for legs wobbled over to the mirror in the bathroom. "No! No!" I cried inwardly to the travesty of a man who looked out at me, "this is not the kisser of one about to pass to his reward day after tomorrow." I leaned close and pulled my eyelids down and then let them flip back. They looked as if they had just been dipped in iodine. But still not like eyes that would be forever closed day after tomorrow with a question mark for a face. (Pay no attention to this: ours is a family of phrase coiners.) I went back to bed and slept soundly.

Well, the fact that I am able to write these older words two weeks later will at last end the horrible suspense and permit you a heavy sigh of relief. I'm not dead, true, but I am not happy. I am worried. I am worried because I was not worried when the jovial Swiss told me I had to go. Why? How could I knock off witticisms right after my sentence of doom? Gallant sallies in the face of death, philosophic last words interspersed, for friends to say, "God, what *je ne sais quois* he always had!"

There must be something wrong with me and I am also worried just how to start in with the psychiatrist who is coming tomorrow.

That entry and reaction became some kind of key, for me at least, as I observed his cavortings with Dhondi. His indifference to life or death might have been the most vital aspect of his "living it up." It was his response to all that had happened.

Dhondi was fourteen when they met.

He had been accused of statutory rape in 1942, tried and acquitted. But it had been the greatest single event in his life. It had occurred at a high point in his cinema career: he had already made *Robin Hood,* a dozen other films. He was world famous.

With time I learned that, in flouncing about the world with Dhondi, he was defying the fates, thumbing his nose at society, at courts, at life itself.

All right, his actions said, you gave me the name, now I'll play the game.

He enjoyed defying the whole world, the laws of organized society. He was going to be guilty of this kind of "rape" (a young, loving, willing girl) publicly day after day.

He was getting even. Los Angeles politicians had jumped on him; he felt they had used him as a pawn in their rivalry with Hollywood film power, made a goat out of him, wrecked his image, prevented him from being famed primarily as an actor, and had hung an albatross of real or alleged criminality upon him.

He couldn't forget it: it had altered his life, the meaning of his days.

So now, to hell with them all, defy fate. That was the real meaning of his cavorting with Dhondi.

We were in a cove in the Rio Grande River, water about eighteen feet. Errol was trying to make an underwater diver out of Dhondi.

I was paddling about on the bamboo raft waiting for

them to return to the raft and continue down river.

Errol placed the gear over Dhondi's head and began dunking her under water. She screamed with fright, surfaced and declared, "Lemme alone!"

He put the gear back over her head, told her how to relax and breathe, dunked her again despite her flapping arms and resisting torso, and held her down. She was below water threshing her arms, trying to escape his grasp and surface.

On surfacing she tore off the headgear, swore and screamed at him, but he persisted.

That went on for about twenty minutes.

He failed, as he had failed before with others. Errol often tried to make athletes out of his girls, but it was a lost cause. "A few," he said, "can hit a tennis ball."

Watching this man live and die—he was doing both at the same time, each quite visibly—was an intense drain on my energies. My own lifestyle was totally different. It was more sedentary, fitting one who is an appendage to a typewriter. Now I was flung into the presence of an unattached meteor wandering through a Caribbean wind.

Errol was thinking about his autobiography in a concentrated way. He was desperate to get it underway, to feel that it was moving. For a time he worried about this method of operating: talking his story out to someone and letting that one do the writing.

He tried talking about himself when he was sober, with no liquor in him. That method failed. He couldn't seem to talk, he was tongue-tied, his mind wouldn't go, his hands trembled, his voice chattered, his memory wouldn't function. We tried that only a few times.

Once or twice a week when he had a drug in him his thoughts flowed, he talked freely and recalled extensively. Moreover, he had been influenced by Thomas De Quincey's *Confessions of an English Opium Eater.* That book has had some vogue in the past century or two as a confession and as a product of a doped-up intelligence.

There have been a few writers since who have fancied that under the influence of hallucinatory drugs they would be able to write ultra-valuably or poetically. Practically all these efforts have failed. Once, back in Hollywood, soon after his rape case, when Errol took to drugs, he also took to writing, hoping that the opiates would heighten his literary faculties.

There is no sign that drugtaking helped him in any way with his writing.

On many of these occasions when I knew he had received a shot he seemed calm, reflective, recollective. If the doctor arrived in the afternoon, Errol worked in the afternoon. If he arrived at night, Errol worked at night: always opening up a few minutes after the man left. Then he would sit easily in his chair or recline in bed, and the words would roll from him about his life in New Guinea or Hollywood, Marseilles or Paris.

I didn't have to question him much then. The flow was his own, the story his own, the mood his own. He would talk for an hour or two and spin one of his stories, the drug apparently helping in the excavation of what those experiences had been.

No, he took the book with an enormous seriousness, more I suspect than he did any film he was ever in and with more real concern than I ever heard him express for any woman.

He would brook no interference from a young nonun-
derstanding female who wanted his attentions, his love-
making, his favors, his services all the time. I was always
aware of the static in the background: the neglected child,
as it were.

He worked, in a certain way, double time.

He would think about what he was going to talk about or
recall it as we moved about the island or as he woke with
thoughts from his sleep at night. I would ask him about
some detail and he might say, "We'll think about that and
get to it later." Or remark, "Today we'll talk about films,"
or "Let's go back to the Sepik River." The memories rose
within him or as I prodded them to the surface.

I was aware of three symbols in Flynn's life.

There was the question mark on his suitclothes, perhaps
the main symbol of his days—to me, in the beginning,
merely a stitching he wore, a peculiarity.

There was the sign of a rooster—he told me about that
—on the flag and the shipside of the *Zaca*. That signified
his captaincy of the female world, his sex symbol. He had
chosen to put a rooster on the ship when he bought it, and
that stemmed from his having settled for the sex reputation
that Hollywood and the world placed upon him after his
rape case.

The third symbol was the sword cane. It always stood in
a corner of the room, lifeless but alive, waiting for him to
pick it up and move out into the world with it.

He came by the use of and the carrying of a cane very
early in life, the same cane that, in one form or another, he
carried all of his days.

Midshipman Young reportedly captured a sword from

Captain Bligh, and the sword remained in Errol's family. The sword landed in their house in Tasmania, and as a small boy Errol played with it as his mother told him its history. The tip of the sword came through the scabbard and there was some writing on the handle. Later his father gave this sword as a souvenir to the Naval and Military Club at Hobart. There it hangs to this day. Errol was angry about that, Professor Flynn wrote to me.

In early photographs of Errol as a young man lording it over New Guinea natives, recruiting them as plantation hands or using them in his search for gold at Edey Creek, tales he has told in *Wicked Ways,* and in his letters to his father in the late 1920s, we see him on the flatlands of New Guinea posed with a cane that has an ordinary curved handle. He walked always and everywhere with this cane. It was a cane he carried also as a cadet officer with the Australian police force assigned to patrol New Guinea territory. The cane gave him an imposing air, the look of a sure-of-himself white Britisher, a man with a manner, a carriage and a meaning. It gave him confidence. In his mind he was seeing in the cane he sported some likeness to the sword that Midshipman Young took from Captain Bligh, the sword that had for him a personal significance. He was a young man trying to find a private style of his own, and he had a good instinct for it.

By the time he was on board his ships, the *Maski* and the *Sirocco,* he always carried a walking cane. Never without it. All the early photographs of him show him with this.

But the cane changed character after he became a Hollywood star. Now he carried a real sword cane. It was a sidearm 2½ feet long, rather rusty at the time we were researching. Still, I would hate to have the tip end of it run through me. The sword was in a rippled, dark-brown hard-wood scabbard. It had a rough-hewn look. On its handle was a tiger's head, and the eyes were supposed to have two diamonds. But one diamond was missing by the time I arrived on the scene, so the badge of rank was now a one-eyed tiger.

Errol carried this sword when he went anywhere—on the plane to Jamaica, about the Titchfield and about Port Antonio, and later as we walked in the streets of Manhattan. Sometimes I saw him take the cane when he went from his room down to the hotel porch for lunch. It is not easy to convey how the cane was an appendage to him, as fitting as one of his limbs, as a leg or an arm. But it was.

He didn't swing it, he didn't handle it in any objectionable way, but in a casual gentlemanly manner. Though it was primarily a symbol, if he ever had to pull the blade out of its sheath and use it, that sword would be useful. Often he unsheathed it just to look at it, or to flash it, or perhaps to regale whomever might be about, but then the long thin line of steel went back into its casing and there it stayed.

When he pulled out that sword and pointed it about with an understated thrust or two, I guess he was really the classic ham. There was a note of threat and danger in the way he did it, as if he were saying: Watch out, this may be meant for you. But just when he would see an uncertain look appear in a viewer's face, he would sheathe the sword again and go about his usually not-so-wicked way.

Errol, carrying a motion picture camera, approached the round table by the pool where I was sitting. He was wearing his regular suit coat and I didn't know why, for he usually moved about the hotel in shorts, shirtless. Even beneath

the suit his squared shoulders gave him a formidable, un-
whippable look. There was an erectness about his head and
neck which was arrogant, a mien that made him special and
recognizable at once. All this came through his dissipated
look, and one accentuated the other.

I was in colorful black-and-red shorts,˙shirtless, taking
the sun.

He handed me the sword. The one gemmed eye of the
tiny tiger head, with the other missing, looked uniquely at
me, I thought, as he said, "Earl, take the sword and cut a
man down with it. I'll film it."

As I went along with most of his shenanigans I took an
appropriate position, so I supposed, the camera already
grinding.

What was I to do? I recalled the romantic scenes where
Errol—or Douglas Fairbanks—slashed their way through
five or ten enemies at a time, leaping on tables and chairs,
clambering up and down ropes, the sidearm flashing.

I unsheathed the blade and whopped it about like an
expert. I stood on the canvas chair and thrust it into some
imaginary enemy's gullet. Ha, now another was coming at
me: I was walled. I stepped higher up on the table and
fought viciously, thrusting that sword once, twice, three
times, knocking off mine enemies. (I am five feet seven and
had then a small black mustache which Errol hated. I
weighed one hundred and forty pounds and could easily
have mimed Charlie Chaplin, and often did.) I flailed away
in some imitation of the cinema greats winning their lady
or saving some Victorian principality from disaster. After I
finished that cavorting (and there were bystanders who
were viewing the performance, I thought with approba-
tion), Errol said, "Now you take a shot of me."

He handed me the camera.

He looked about, stationed himself in a set way, with the ocean and palm trees behind. He nodded his head slightly, the go-ahead to start filming.

He stood for ten or fifteen seconds gazing at nothing, but being Errol Flynn. Then he unsheathed the gleaming steel slowly and with one gesture, or no gesture at all, pointed it straight at me and the camera. He held that pose for half a minute as I filmed away. When the hell was he going to start fighting and mowing down those foreign invaders?

"Cut," he murmured. I stopped shooting.

He lowered the sword and placed it back in its sheath.

Why, the bastard! These two shots would be on the same film, I cavorting like a monkey, he just doing nothing but being the great handsome brute of an Errol Flynn, looking grand, doing nothing but being the incomparable swordsman.

His damned incessant tricks! I didn't know he liked me well enough to want to see me make an ass of myself.

He had a curious idea about what a "scientific" experiment might or ought to be. He believed that the games he played with people, the productions he put on with them, the cat-and-mouse playlets he devised, could or should be viewed as operations of a "scientific" nature. Often when he pranked he would end the prank—after the laughter—with the offhand remark, "Just a scientific experiment, pal."

Maybe he had not changed much, in that respect, from the time when he was a small boy in Tasmania. At the age of seven he had made the experiment of feeding one duck a string with a piece of fat on it (which went through the duck almost instantly, Errol said), then placing the fat and string into the bill of another duck until he had seven or eight ducks connected and waddling about. That stunt, which he called "the only living bracelet," struck his father as an act of cruelty toward the ducks, and his father swatted Errol with an umbrella. Errol said it was the only act of violence against him ever by his father. The boy had gone on scientific trips with his father: he had simply picked up an erroneous notion of what an experiment might be.

His subsequent "experiments" never changed character very much from that original one.

He never got off the ground as a scientist. Neither did he ever get over imagining that he was, in some part, a scientist. It was, of course, the influence of his father. But Errol's science was always some stunt that was half-theater, half-nonsense. Outrage somebody and then study the reaction. He did this with actors, women, aides, flunkies, collaborators, even his parents.

When people reacted sharply and jumped out of their skins, he stood back and watched the upset; then he always began that throaty laugh of his and at the end disposed of the scene by calling it a scientific experiment.

Errol as scientist never achieved or recorded any conclusions from his habit of provoking outrage. Perhaps it is not too farfetched to suggest that his total career was some kind of public outrage, a single man's human experiment with society, as if to test how much the world would put up with. That, in fact, may be the key to why he aroused public interest so intensively.

The point is, Errol was, in some large part, his father's son. Marelle Flynn simply wasn't everything in her son's life. Professor Flynn was famous for having dipped backward into the sea millions of years, for having come up with oceanic species that threw light on evolution, on man's emergence from the sea. He knew the name and identity and something of the history of much that moved in the ocean.

Along comes Errol: a pioneer diver, using tubes and compressed air before the modern equipment to go under water had been invented. And Errol starts going under water, deep down, scores of feet below, down as far as old sunken galleys, searching in rock declivities and in the cliff sides of oceans. He spears the fish, he sees the shark life, startles them and is startled by them, he tangles with octopi, but always manages to come up and breathe air again. A scientist without findings, one might say, but his father's son: a deep-sea diver, a mariner, a goer-below into the world of plankton, starfish, poison-spined creatures of the deep, life that goes back billions of years.

Was Errol trying to match and outdo and one-up his father? Sons have often competed with their fathers.

The malaise that affects many parental-filial relationships among the famed, especially in the cinema and political worlds, may well have been a factor in Errol's drives, aims, competitions. The likelihood is that he really was competing to equal his father's reputation.

I once asked Errol if he felt that his father's work was more or less important than his own. How did he compare his own fifty films, his value as an entertainer, actor, creator, with his father's impact? Errol said he believed that his own career was every bit as important to the world as his father's and might even be more important creatively than what his father had done and had left in the world of science.

If there was a nexus in Errol's career where his sense of competition took off it was in the neglect he experienced when his parents dropped him off at a private school called Southwest London College, between Putney and Hammersmith, a suburb of London. Neglect, a famous parent overshadowing a growing son or daughter, is well known to often take a toll, to lead to upset lives in the offspring, to crime, wildness, suicides, public escapades. Maybe they are striking back for being overshadowed and neglected.

Errol, as a parent, may have repeated the same neglect after he fathered four children with whom he spent little time. "How could I?" he said to me once when I asked him about this. "My work has taken me around the globe. I couldn't be a house papa." He had to go on making movies, money, fame, and he saw little of his three daughters and son Sean. Sean tried, sadly, to duplicate his father. He was in a film, *Son of Captain Blood,* a motion picture that failed. While Errol could go to Spain and Cuba and come back alive—he was such a tough survivalist—Sean, who went to Cambodia as a photographer during the Vietnam War, never returned. The hard drives, the tough youth that was in back of Errol, may not have been there in the upbringing of Sean. But the paternal neglect was in part similar to what Errol had experienced.

I was up early, ready to start work. I heard him moving about in his room and knocked. He said come in.

For Errol it wasn't the sun that rose in the morning. Daylight was a curtain that went up, and as he climbed out of bed his first steps were as an entrance upon a stage or a studio set. The world was the scene that would be shot today, and he would be actor and perhaps cameraman, director and producer besides.

Each morning he and the world met upon this principle.

He went to a table on which rested two breakfast plates, with scrambled eggs, coffee asteam, and in the center of the table a bowl of fruit. He stood at the table an instant, then picked up a dab of egg with the thumb and forefinger of his right hand and chucked it into his mouth. So much for the eggs. His hand groped toward the fruit bowl. There was a bunch of grapes at the top and he twisted off three of them and chucked them into his open mouth. He looked about for something else. His glance settled on a small table in a corner. Ah, that was it. There a bottle of vodka stood, waiting for his attention, a tall glass beside it. He poured the vodka into the glass full up, sprinkled about an eighth of an inch of tonic over that, lifted the glass to his lips and took a small sip. That was his breakfast. Then he turned to me.

I never saw him eat any more than that for breakfast, and I never saw him begin the day in any way other than a tall shot of vodka with an eighth inch of tonic over it.

He sat sipping. He had the chatters badly. His fingers shook in a way beyond imagery to paint. His eyes seemed small, his cheekbones swollen; there were layers of fat along his ribs. He looked like the drunk in the movie of *The Sun Also Rises.*

It was a warm morning. He perspired, kept drinking, perspired more, struggled to tell of an event in Paris with his first wife many years earlier. He couldn't talk. I didn't know whether to suggest postponing the work.

Let him make the move. I thought he might. I had seen this before.

But the man was trying to get to his story. I knew how

much his autobiography meant to him: it was like worrying about an epitaph.

Of a sudden he said, "Let's quit. Let's go out on the water."

I was glad not to have to work with him in that condition.

"We'll motorboat to Castle Comfort," he said. That was about twelve miles away.

Williams came by with the boat. It was big enough to seat eight or ten: a long boat, with a motor that worked much of the time. Williams would run the motor, steer the craft, Small Companion and I would be seated on the crosspieces. Errol would stand forward, pointing ahead or obliqueward the direction Williams should take up the coast.

We went in and out of bays and inlets, over reefs and shoals.

Quiet trip. I felt something was wrong, that it could not remain this way for too long.

At length we came into the cove that led to the stony shore at the foot of the hill that housed his caretaker's home. Castle Comfort: Flynn country.

We moved from water ninety or a hundred feet deep into shallower water thirty or forty feet. We met up with rollers breaking against stones and boulders. The water became very choppy, the boat rose and fell in a drunken way. Errol seemed to be delighted. The choppy water, the wavering boat was the first exciting thing so far.

We were now in water only ten or fifteen feet deep. The rollers were heavy splash five or six feet high. I wasn't happy. A way of putting it.

Neither was Dhondi.

Errol was wreathed in a smile. He liked the rocking motion, the beating of the rollers on our craft. The boat now seemed very small.

Of a sudden he rocked from side to side, as if shaking the boat and trying to throw it over.

He gave one heavy lurch. The boat turned and we were all in the water. The hull promptly hit me in the skull. I was under water, seeing the upturned boat, oars floating about, making out one or two people above and, as I thought, a big fish below. My lungs were filling, my nose felt plugged with the sea and foam.

I tried to grab hold of the boat in its upside-down position, grabbed the gunwale. The boat turned over, the hull up again. I was under water again.

Williams had secured Dhondi and placed her across the rounded top. Now he was going for me. Jamaica is filled with beautifully built young black men very much at home in the water, highly muscular and good swimmers. I too was soon atop that overturned boat, grim of face, saved by Williams.

Errol helped push the boat, still upside down, closer to shore. Dhondi and I were riding on top of the overturned craft in only two or three feet of water.

We scrambled onto the stony beach and staggered up on the sand.

On the beach, sprawled on sand and stones, Errol said: "Not a chance of anything happening, sport. Not a chance. I was there. Williams was there. The water was only fifteen feet deep. We had our eyes on you all the time."

"I thought I saw a shark below me," I said.

"That was me," he said. "I was below crawling on the bottom laughing at you and Dhondi up there floundering in the water."

"Laughing? Under water?"

"Yes, I was laughing."

I wondered whether I would get pneumonia or heart failure.

"You understand," he reminded me as he had done before, "I only do things like that with and to people I like. There's no fun in unsettling a stranger. You get nothing out of that. It's when you undo or unsettle or shake up a friend that it's great to watch."

And I ask you, what better friend than that does one need?

By now I was developing a wary fondness for him.

Back at the Titchfield a couple of hours later I beheld something I hadn't suspected: that he was virtually friendless.

The mail arrived.

I had a pile of it from family and friends, personal notes of no consequence, merely close ones keeping in touch with me, wondering how I fared with the famed Flynn and telling me what they did in their teaching jobs, or insurance offices, or literary work, or goings on in my neighborhood in Manhattan. A packet of seven or eight such letters, meaningful only to me. I would usually grab them, retire to my room, read them, think back a moment upon the New York scene and toss the letters into a suitcase.

As I picked up that day's bundle of letters Errol said, "Jesus, look at the mail that guy gets."

I was shocked. I realized then that the man heard from hardly anyone, that his mail was limited to a letter from his lawyer, a request from an organization for him to lend his name to some medical or political cause, once in a while a straight piece of junk mail, and a phone call perhaps from his current wife asking for some money: little else.

I decided then and there I would never be around when the mail arrived, never again let him see me get that cluster of personal notes filled with trivia—perhaps the trivia of real existence—while he received nothing but once, for example, a list mentioning his name as being on a blacklist prepared by the Screen Writers Guild.

I recall only one significant letter he received during all the time I was with him in Jamaica. It was from someone in a jail in Louisiana, a dark man who had been one of the crew on board his *Zaca*. "A good fellow, a nice young chap," said Errol. "He worked hard, he was smart."

Now he wrote that he was spending twenty years in a prison in Louisiana and wanted help in getting out.

"Twenty years!" I exclaimed. "What did he do?"

"They found some marijuana dust in his pants pocket."

"What do you mean, dust?"

"Just that, not even a cigarette of it. Just a tiny amount located by microscope, tested out and found to be the residue of a pinch or two of marijuana."

"Twenty years for that?"

"Twenty years."

"You mean the State of Louisiana is willing to support this man and tax the taxpayers of that state for twenty years for having a few grains of that weed on him?"

"That must be it, nothing else."

"What can you do?"

"Write to the Governor. I'll sign it. Tell him this young fellow was of good character, that he worked for me, that twenty years seems a long time to have to be in jail for a thing like that."

I mused aloud. "It seems to me I've heard something like this about someone else somewhere. Where was it? What was it?"

"You are thinking of Jean Valjean in *Les Miserables,* pursued by the French inspector, Javert, for stealing a loaf of bread."

"That must be it. Twenty years for a few grams of smoke."

"That's what's going on, that's the world we live in. I smoke the stuff and people laugh at it or the law ignores it and I get away with it. But they are death on ganja here in Jamaica and in some other parts of the world."

"But it took a microscope to find it, you say. . . ."

"Yes . . . twenty years."

I wrote a letter to the Governor of Louisiana. Errol signed it.

We never heard the outcome.

Errol was busy going on to other things in the coming days: New York, Cuba, Hollywood . . . Vancouver.

This man to be so isolated?

Yet it was true.

Some people, when they achieve unexcelled heights, can find themselves in an isolated position. It is a condition that has been commented upon in the lives of the celebrated, especially cinema heroes, whose fame is largely made-to-order: made by media, promotion, advertising, newspaper stories, by all the instruments of legend-making. This process of hero-creating can be the undoing of the hero himself.

One morning about eleven o'clock—we were ordinarily at work an hour before this—I chanced upon him near the receptionist's desk in the lobby. Dhondi was with him. His face was set, serious, cold.

"Ready to work, Errol?"

"We . . . I've been meaning to talk to you about that." Somber, resonant voice, touch of warning in it.

I waited.

"I, ah, think . . . it seems to me . . . well, no, we won't be working."

A timed silence.

"What's the matter?" Inside I was quaking a bit.

"I, ah, it seems to me . . . I'm not sure the work is going exactly . . . well, I don't think . . ."

I wondered about my color.

Dhondi looked on seriously. His mood was deepening. He was registering dissatisfaction with me, with the progress of his story. I thought he was a bit nasty, too.

He fidgeted, as if the task was most unpleasant. "Maybe," he ventured, hesitated, "maybe a younger man . . . a . . ."

"WHAT THE HELL IS THIS?" That was a roar from me.

He carried on, raised his voice. "You're always at the swimming pool," he complained. It sounded strangely anticlimactic to me.

He let the moment hang, like an actor timing his flow of speech so the audience will secure the right wallop.

He turned to Dhondi. "Dhondi, did you do as I told you? Did you arrange for Conrad's flight back to the States?"

I stepped toward him. "What's the matter with the way the work is going?"

Errol looked at Dhondi. She looked at him. Both deadly serious.

I had something more to say. "I can get my own ticket if I have to!" I glared at Dhondi. She didn't look any better to me than did Errol.

Suddenly he seemed to be heaving with laughter; he slapped his right thigh, something I rarely saw him do.

Dhondi went into a hysterical fit of laughter.

He acted as if he were trying to catch his breath, it was so funny. "You never can . . ." he started stammering, as his laughter declined. "You never can tell what's in a guy . . ." laughter . . . "till you test him."

One of his goddamned "scientific" experiments. Another one!

I let him have it.

"DON'T—EVER—DO—THAT—AGAIN!"

This time his face went serious, his mouth opened slightly, his chin dropped. I watched with anger, not with glee.

He sized me up as thin-skinned and never did pull one of his pranks on me again. At least not a serious one. He was thereafter always sensitive, even to what Dhondi had to say to me.

In fact, from that time on he seemed anxious to shield me from all blows whatever, from anywhere.

In the limousine he explained he was going to meet with his plantation help, and I recollected his statement to the Jamaica *Gleaner* about doing something for his employees.

High up on a hill, where rambling, rickety roadways took us, was the small place he called Castle Comfort. There his caretaker lived. The house was no castle but a simple one-story home from which the caretaker ran the Flynn estate, or plantation, or acreage or whatever the great land was that ran for two miles along the north coast.

We stepped out of the car and walked a few rods to the rear of the house. There stood a gathering of about twenty of Errol's serfs, or workers or whatever they were, waiting for him, as they had been told to do. He was to speak to them today and would do things for them, they had been told, and as it said in the newspaper he would listen to what the people wanted.

I stood fifteen feet away, watching a modern man in one of his settings: his great property, the accumulation of his life in films and in finance.

He spoke for a few minutes and I didn't seem to be listening much. I was always enamored of the view of the Atlantic spilling away into the horizon, and the curious plants of the region attracted my eye. Frangipani plant was everywhere, and a growth called bougainvillea, and I looked over the ferns and thickets, and what seemed to be some plowed-up land: and there was this animal that looked like a hog, huge, with a horn atop his head. I had never seen a hog with, if that is what it was, a black horn, threatening all comers with this curved weapon at the top of its skull.

The animal glared at me with hatred as I studied him. He wanted to gore me but didn't dare charge. His eyes were black, human, intelligent, and they flared hatred, hatred of all the two-leggeds who seemed to run things, who tilled the soil, who killed the fowl and who occasionally took a small pig off never to be seen again. I was so interested in that animal, weighing several hundred pounds, that I wasn't listening to Errol as he proposed to his help a pension plan if they stayed long enough in his service. Ten more years, twenty years, whatever it was: they would be retired and they would have a pension.

There was a hullabaloo among them and I turned my attention back to Errol. The hands were surrounding him, each talking, registering some kind of complaint. They were pressing him backward: men and women, all black, and one woman was saying, "My boy pick lime every day five day week and he get one shilling. Give him dem pension money now, two shilling." It shocked me into alertness.

I heard another complaint, again a woman; she picked something else, citrus, breadfruit or plantain and she worked all week for not quite a pound (two dollars and eighty cents) "and that why we teefing. If we don teef we cahnt live." Teefing. The word came to me, a Jamaica contraction of thieving. They were openly saying that if they did not steal the produce they didn't have enough to eat. Others kept saying that they had to "teef" off the field if they were to make ends meet and have food on the table. They had to teef a chicken, teef a hog, teef the breadfruit, "Because you don pay us what to eat."

The litany went on, painful to him, for ten minutes, fifteen minutes. I was embarrassed. He looked my way once or twice.

I moved away. I went into the house and talked with the caretaker.

The caretaker said, "I don't know why he did this. I don't know why he called this meeting. I don't know what he had in mind. I don't know what he expected to accomplish. He's not going to give them more money. They are jumping all over him. He should have known if he ever confronted them they would do this. They never see him. They see him only from a distance when he rarely gets out here. Now he has this meeting and they are jumping on him. He should have stayed away. I knew this would happen. I knew it, I knew it."

The caretaker went on that way. I peered out the window at the milling scene. They didn't want to hurt him. They just wanted him to know since he had said he would be of help. They seemed to be bending him backward toward the caretaker's house in their vehemence. He was close to the house now, rattled, ashen, saying little, wanting to be away.

The caretaker went out and stood between Errol and the workers. "The meeting is over," the caretaker said. "Mr. Flynn will think about what you say." Errol said he would think about it. He was backing off. We were all backing off toward the car.

The hands drifted off in different directions, back to their tasks, their lime picking, climbing the copra trees. They moved off in twos and threes in varying directions back across the estate.

The strange moment was over. It was embarrassing to me, unsettling to him.

The meeting was a howling failure.

I took another look at that ugly horned animal.

Errol was quiet, depressed, all the way back to the hotel.

Somewhere en route to Jamaica, maybe on the airtrip down, Errol had come up with that pension idea. Maybe his Jamaica lawyer had mentioned the possibility to him sometime in the past. Maybe he was trying to prove to himself that he wasn't all that indifferent to the people who drudged for him.

But he was trapped between his touch of benevolence and the realities of employment in Jamaica, where field serfs were abundant, work was scarce, a pound a week was big money and two pounds was tops for a secretary. Maybe he was trapped by his own need for incessant aggrandizement, as are all the mighty. Maybe he was afraid someone —perhaps a lawyer—would one day take all this away from him. Someone would take it away as people had taken things from him before. He had, after all, gone through eight million bucks. It hadn't all gone on drinks, dope and women. Lots of it was seized from him by finance types like himself, a business manager, lawyers, others.

He had tried to do something for his help, within the limits of his time and place and finances, but he was himself apparently a trapped victim of his well-meant effort.

We motorboated across the channel that separated the mainland of Jamaica, at Port Antonio, from a green unpeopled spot of land called Navy Island. The island was a roll of hills covered with jungle growth, and there were a few stony paths or ridges over which Errol led me.

As we strolled and, with machetes, struck away from us branches and ferns, Errol told me of a dog who lived two thousand years ago for which he had a certain love: the dog and what happened to it touched his heartstrings.

I knew by now, from other stories he told me, that he loved dogs. One of the earliest photos shows him at the age of four in front of a tent, a pirate ship in the rear, and he is Robinson Crusoe and the dog at his side is named Friday. Later he had dogs with him on board each of his sailboats. He had one dog he called Cold Nose and a dog in New Guinea named Picnis. He had a dog, Arno, at Mulholland House in Hollywood. He referred to some of his dogs also as small companions.

He believed that a dog had a certain place and role and

should be controllable. He had the same notion about servants and women. Things, people, dogs had to be kept in
line. If they got out of line, give them the treatment that the
famed Mexican artist, Diego Rivera, urged upon him. Rivera had told him that women must be treated coldly, bru-
tally.

I was astounded to learn this as I had admired Rivera's
work and watched him, when I was young, painting a huge
mural in an old building in Lower New York. Rivera had
identified himself with one of the numerous political fac-
tions of the day, and to see him paint, with the assistance
of a few students, and to hear him lecture about Socrates,
was to think and believe you were in the presence of a great
humanitarian. But in Mexico the artist told Errol to be
hardboiled with women and keep them where they belonged—wherever that was. So women, dogs and servants
had to do what he expected or Errol could land on them.

Seven or eight years earlier, when he was in Italy, he said,
he was wandering about the streets of Pompeii by himself.
A rain had made gutters of the ancient chariot furrows,
worn half a foot into hard rock. He had to proceed hurriedly in a series of leaps to keep his feet dry and try to find
cover to avoid the watchmen whom he knew would want to
toss him out of the city. At four o'clock the six gates of
Pompeii swing shut to visitors and those inside are supposed to get out, he explained, but that was the time of
evening when Errol liked Pompeii best. Then he could
imagine what it might have been like in A.D. 79, before
disaster struck the place.

He decided to head for the Museum of Pompeii, which
he had never visited before. He had a mystic feeling as he
reached the stone blocks that led to the barracks of the
gladiators. The element of time took on another dimen-

sion, and he was moved at finding himself alone there, reliving that crucial moment of the past.

It was almost dark when he groped his way down some stone steps. He knew vaguely where the museum was, just past the ancient thermal baths, cleverly disguised and constructed for the use of both men and women. Soon he had the museum in view. It was a long tunnel-like structure, rather like a windowless subway, he said, filled with glass cases. In these lay the casts of human corpses, ancient Pompeians grotesquely contorted in their death agonies, pathetic and gruesome records of the horrors of the great eruption.

Not only people died, Errol said, but there in the dark by the eerie light of his cigarette lighter he looked into the last glass case and there was a dog. "A large dog, this one, lean and whipcorded and you'd guess with short bristly hair, powerfully built too, yet with long sinewy legs that could carry him swiftly on the chase. But it was his head, like a cheetah, that fascinated me. It was wide, much too wide and too big for his body. In death the lips were drawn back in a snarl as if even in his last suffocating agonies he defied the unknown enemy that was killing him."

Errol went on, seeing that dog's face once more. "The timing did him wrong except—poor guy—he might have escaped but that he had been chained up. The chain and collar were still on and I will never forget the wild stare in his fierce eyes, the savage bewilderment at this choking death."

Yes, Errol could be much moved by dogs, even by one that lived two thousand years ago.

This man could love that dog, yet there is another dog story that lies farther ahead and is different. . . .

•   •   •

Back at the hotel—we weren't working much this day—
Errol suggested we go down into town, into the market
square, where anything that might be doing about town
would be doing.

It was unusual for the townspeople, virtually all black, to
see the great Fleen (as they pronounced him) strolling
about looking at the fruit stands, stocks of sewing materials,
gadgets for the house, pans and the like.

The square was about forty yards across each way. People milled in that area as they passed from one stand to
another looking over the articles for sale.

As "Fleen" and I entered the marketplace and passed
from one stand to another, word spread: Look who's here.
Fleen and his lawyer. They thought of me as his lawyer. (A
man like him, they figured, had to move around with a
lawyer from minute to minute.)

A calypso band located in the marketplace to liven
things up for the buyers (the musicians were paid by the
merchants) struck up, playing *Wukkin for the Yankee
Dollah.*

At once Errol grabbed my hand and started swinging me
about the square to the rhythm of the power of the *Yankee
Dollah.*

I had little awareness of what I was doing. I was being
swung around that circle on Errol's volition. We whirled
about, Errol and I, he looking like Nureyev and me a bit like
Charlie Chaplin.

But in a few minutes everybody was adance, all of us
together in a circle, swinging around and around to various
calypso tunes. For once in the history of Port Antonio, the
town was nighttime by day.

•   •   •

A lively prospect had been brewing for some time: a day at the races. Errol owned a racetrack and on a certain day each year races were held, prizes were awarded, betting was allowed: and a portion of North Jamaica turned out for the affair.

I had never seen the racetrack. It was located in an inner recess of his estate. But now I was there with him, going through bush, brush, weed, roaches and semiroads to a fenced-in area.

Inside the wire fence was the racetrack, about a hundred and fifty yards around and fifty yards across at its widest diameter. It was egg-shaped.

Here, after publishing three million words in book form, I am at a loss for descriptive language to describe what was inside that fence. I'll try.

All about the edge of the egg just inside the fence was a path, reasonably sandy and unreasonably rocky. At points it was twenty feet wide, but mostly ten or twelve feet wide. This is where the horses would run. Inside the egg were trees, cacti, shrubbery, fern, rocks—and finally this one feature: the whole track was on the side of a slope. As the horse and rider ran down one stretch of the track they turned and moved up on the other side of the egg, about thirty feet higher. So you could see the whole race at all times: the lower edge of the egg if you were close up and the side or ridge of the racetrack higher up on the inside of that fence. The main thing you saw at the upper edge of the egg or oval was that wire fence through which horse and rider were not supposed to go.

Races were already on when we got there.

You could follow the horses and racers around that oval almost as rapidly as your eyes could sweep over a plate of soft-boiled eggs for breakfast in the morning.

The features of the place didn't end there.

At one end of the track was a stand, like a lighthouse, forty feet in the air. Up there the officials fired their shots and set off the horses. You could see them from half a mile away officiating.

On all sides of the oval or racetrack or improvisation, or whatever it was, thousands of Jamaicans scrambled over each other to watch the proceedings: repeated short races lasting half a minute or a minute, or three times around the track for a longer race. And then a winner, then a prize, then another shot.

But there is more. The explanation is that the racetrack was built in equatorial jungle: it was carved out of masses of foliage such as only Rousseau could paint or conceive. Somehow tractors and men had worked for the famous handicapper at some time or other and built this racetrack right out of that jungle.

Moreover, the racetrack could at times be dismantled. Then the whacked-out area, insofar as the jungle was whacked out of it, acted as an airplane landing for Errol or one of his Hollywood pilots who might fly down in a Cessna and have to land someplace.

Watching the races was a little like watching a tennis game. As the horses, usually four to a race, started out, moving away from you, they went so fast and had such a short distance to go to get to the other end that your head was already revolving about following them, and as they came back, moving up and around the slope above, your head was still revolving, left-right left-right—and somebody had won.

After an hour and a half of that and much horn blowing and many shots, Errol and I took leave of the track.

Errol, known all over the world as an enthusiast of the horseracing profession, had spent a huge gob of dough to get that runway going so that once a year there was an Errol Flynn Day in Jamaica and races around that oversized egg.

It was one more wonderful treat—I am serious about that —of the many things I had been promised. No one ever accused Errol of unoriginality.

On that day he lost no money betting. "I don't bet at my own racetrack," he said.

"What happens to those horses?" I asked.

"They wind up in cans of dogfood that are sold in the United States."

"Really?"

"Sure, you don't think I regard that investment as a racetrack, do you?"

It was the dogs that got gypped. The horses were primarily bones. I never saw a muscle on a single horse and couldn't figure how they could run. If four horses were flying close together they looked like War, Famine, Pestilence and Death.

Errol fancied himself an expert in wines and liquors and knowledgeable about the foods of many lands. It seemed a form of intellectualization for him to expatiate on these fine points. This is often an indulgence of the traveled who can talk of restaurants, foods, spices, rare vintages. Sometimes they confuse this superficiality with significant knowledge and project it as a sign of their culture.

Errol had a fair share of this. Perhaps he had more right than most because he had seen more of the world than most, and he had lived inside many lands.

In a way this diversity could be his undoing, anyone's

undoing, and one day he was nearly undone. We thought we lost him.

He had gone on one of these gourmet talk binges, boasting his knowledge of the wines of France, telling some tale of an ancient East Indian wine with gold specks in it, and passing from food to food. His eyes rolled in the storied manner of the poet's fine frenzy as he fed me this fount of his experience, and he wound up saying, "I shall call Randolph and order for lunch raw hamburger with egg yolk. It's a rare dish."

At one o'clock, after he and I had talked for about three hours, we adjourned to Errol's table on the dining porch. When Randolph appeared Errol gave him direction. "Now I want the ground meat to be raw, ground finely. Let there be two egg yolks, no white of the egg, in the center of the meat. Press the center of the meat with a tablespoon, drop the yolks in there. Let there be plenty of pepper on the table."

Soon the special dish came, with leaves of greenery around the edges of the platter. It looked forbidding to me.

With an air of pomp, and as if about to teach me something, he dug his fork into the hamburger. The center of it was a sickly gray. "Don't call it hamburger," he corrected.

Now they do not get meat or much of it in Jamaica, and whatever they had in the way of meat was dubious. They had lean, scrawny, bony cattle in Jamaica that didn't make much good meat. Beef was imported for people in the hotels in Kingston or Ocho Rios, and it wasn't much good for them either. This was a fruit- and produce-eating land: breadfruit, grapefruit, eggs, akee, some chicken and more breadfruit, some fish (also imported from Canada), and the people were largely toothless.

"Errol," I said, "that meat looks like hell. You sure you know what you're doing? Look at the color of it."

He dabbled at the raw egg, mixed it with spoonful after spoonful of the gray meat. He seemed to be working at it as if to prove something.

I thought that, before my eyes, his appetite waned. His color changed. I ventured, "Let it go, Errol. Eat a banana."

He plunged on through most of the plate, about a pound of the meat. Then he got up from the table remarking, "I've had it."

He busied himself all afternoon trying to work off the combination of food he had taken in. We went boating, we swam. He took in more vodka than usual. Usually he took it from a glass, but as we boated around, he swigged it from a bottle.

I figured he was putting in his usual defying-the-normal day. He might even get away with that scrummy luncheon.

In the evening he wanted no food. But he smoked, drank and stayed in bed and tried to read. He monkeyed with his tape recorder for a while. Then a big red blotch broke out on his face. He began to perspire; under the blotch his color whitened.

Dhondi and I watched in alarm.

I phoned a doctor who lived a few minutes away and told him of the raw meat. The physician, a black Jamaican who knew Errol very well, advised, "Get Epsom salts, a large dose, make him take it. I'll be right over. It sounds like food poisoning. That foolish man."

I went down to the kitchen of the hotel. It was ten o'clock at night. Nobody was there. I had never been in the kitchen before. I put on the electric light. It was a large kitchen with about thirty individual cupboards all along one wall, with pull-out drawers that swung downward. Inside each drawer were sugar, salt, butter, cheese, pepper, curry, oregano, and so on through thirty or more labels on the outside of each drawer.

I found nothing that said Epsom salts, but I began opening each drawer, pulling down each board to see what was inside.

I nearly fainted.

Over the cheese that I ate each day were thousands of roaches, swarming, feeding, living happily ever after. God!

I opened the one labeled sugar. Thousands and thousands of roaches three and four inches deep over the sugar. The roaches clambered over each other but did not fight and claw. I have never seen two roaches fight each other.

Now, from curiosity and fury, I opened each of the thirty drawers. Over everything hundreds of thousands of roaches. Big ones.

Over all the food that I and others ate three times a day, but when the food was taken out it was brought to the table roachless.

Migod, Jamaica! This hotel!

I remembered what some Jamaican said to me about roaches, "Dem roach keepen everything clean."

Little knowledge here of how disease spreads; that, or a great rationalization.

I felt almost as sick as was Errol.

I moved out of the kitchen, back up the stairs, without Epsom salts, without anything.

The doctor was there. He gave Errol a shot of adrenalin, and he may have done other things. I was in a dither trying to stay about and trying to keep away.

The physician was there half an hour. He murmured,

"No one can do much for him. He either lives or dies."

Errol was lying there now, quieter, his face looking like German measles, his whole body a breakout of angry poisonous matter.

I stayed at his bedside till one or two o'clock. So did Dhondi. Finally she said, "I think you can go to bed now. Maybe he'll get through it. I think he will."

"Call me if you need help." I was in the next room.

I stayed awake, fighting off mosquitoes that were biting me savagely and thinking of those roaches that were over all that food, running through the flour, wallowing in the ginger, more gourmet than Flynn, even less particular, and able to thrive on any vegetable and animal matter in the world.

I thought of how the roaches cluttered up the ground beneath your footing as you walked in the Jamaica fields.

The roaches lived here.

They loved it.

So did Errol.

After the second day Errol began ordering around the help in an imperious way and I knew we would have another chance to get at his life story.

Just when he was surviving one food adventure, but not out of it yet, still another arrived his way.

It was morning, the third day after his attack; he was sitting up in bed, still taking in all kinds of drinks, soft ones, lemonade, coffee, plain water even—when we heard an auto roll into the yard below his quarters.

In a minute or two a black chauffeur knocked on Errol's door.

"A gift from Mrs. Rixmann," he said, handing Dhondi a

glass jar half filled with something very red.

Errol exlaimed, "Hannah's escargot!"

It sounded to me like a cry from the crow's nest of the *Bounty.*

He sat up sharply. "Get me a spoon, someone."

I asked what it was.

"Snails."

Forgive me, God, for my ignorance: I didn't know escargot was French for snails. I have been such an uncosmopolitan all my life.

"Snails! You eat snails?"

"Certainly. Delicious."

"But Errol," I remonstrated, "you've just escaped the grimmest reaper of all from that raw-meat and egg-yolk delight. This is no time to . . ."

He had downed several of them by now; the spoon was dipping lower into that red muck.

Realizing that he would survive this and it might even be the best medicine for him, and playing his prankster's game, I fled from the room yelling that I would personally go get the physician this time.

In a few hours Errol was down at the pool swimming underwater, back and forth, splashing up waves in whale-like spouts.

What do you do with a guy like that?

As we cavorted about the pool he remarked that in a few days we would all go visit Hannah Rixmann. "My best friend," he informed me.

For days after seeing that ocean of roaches I couldn't eat. I stuck with boiled eggs, fresh fruit that I opened with a knife when it was brought to the table whole, a few items out of jars, like jelly, and crackers that I took out of packages gingerly.

My despair was showing. I kept seeing the roaches in their lifetime immersion in the foods, enjoying life in their own brand of roach socialism.

Randolph, the black waiter, spotted my chagrin and decline and noticed how I ordered carefully. He said to me one noon, "You are physically ill, Mr. Conrad?"

"Yes, I am physically ill. Every time I get ill it is a physical illness."

"I am sorry you are physically ill," he said.

"As I say, whenever I get ill it is physical and nothing else. I am that way now. I was disappointed with the kitchen. Do people here all have to contend with those roaches?"

"Oh, it is much cleaner in the hotel kitchen than it is almost anywhere around, in the bars, in the private homes. We and the roaches inhabit Jamaica."

"How come the roaches haven't been given credit?"

He didn't follow my reasoning.

"I hope you soon get over your physical illness."

"When I do," I said, "it won't be physical any longer. Thank you, Randolph."

Errol's attack of ptomaine, or whatever, was forgotten in a few days. His epicure taste remained about the same. He couldn't resist the temptation to taste something new, bitter, spiced. At one luncheon some delicacy that he liked escalated his emotions. Errol hailed Randolph, his musical voice ringing out across the dining area.

Randolph hurried to his side. Eyes were on Errol.

"Randolph, call Celia out here!" He was giving com-

mands as on the *Zaca* or in a film where he might be taking
Burma single-handed.

"Yessir, Mr. Fleen."

"I want to give her kiss."

"You wish to give kiss Celia." It was repeated as question, statement and an order to be obeyed.

"She has made the akee and fish so beautiful today I wish
to give her kiss."

Randolph ran out to the kitchen.

Celia, stout, dark-skinned, aproned, came out to see what
the master wanted. Randolph had not told her the reason
for her command call.

Errol arose, walked two or three steps toward her. "Wonderful akee, Celia." *Smack.* He put his arms around her.
Smack.

From the time when Hannah Rixmann sent over those
chili-drenched snails, he had promised we would motor
across the island to her home and spend a few days there.

We moved in two cars—Errol, Dhondi and myself in one,
the court reporter in his own car. We arrived a few hours
later at a large home situated on a cliff alongside the broad
Caribbean.

For several days we rested, swam, played music, did some
work, ate well. Errol cut down on the drink. I saw he could
go without hard drugs for several days.

Even so, his craving for incessant sensation stayed constant. . . .

No one in the world will believe this story but it happened.

Errol did a dance that can only be called the Chutney
Dervish.

Chutney is a Hindustani word and a Hindustani relish or sauce. It is a hot-tasting condiment of fruit seasoned with chili, garlic, mustard and vinegar.

McDonald's hasn't yet discovered it, to the best of my knowledge, but if they ever do one whole generation will be doing the Chutney Dervish on the streets of the cities of the country.

When you put chutney on your tongue and it reaches your throat, your eyes pop three inches out in front of your forehead and your throat closes up tight as a telephone wire; you get it down and you tell yourself that you've had an East Indian delicacy.

Errol must have discovered it in a whorehouse in Kuala Lumpur or Katmandu.

He usually carried a jar of it with him wherever he went. He couldn't live without it. If anyone wanted a way to his heart or pocketbook they had only to give him this fantastic throat burner, eye glazer and stomach murderer. The East Indians may protest this book and war may break out in the area of Boom La Dash, or wherever they do their fighting over this passage. I can't help it.

On the first day we were there, as Hannah knew was expected, a jar of freshly made chutney was on the table about nine inches from Errol's nose.

He hadn't had any good homemade chutney with the right amounts of vinegar, garlic, mustard and chili in it in weeks or months. I gathered from the performance I was about to see that he had gone without True Chutney for a long time. Maybe he did not have it at all in Africa where he had recently been while making *The Roots of Heaven.*

This jar of chutney was arranged by his friend, made by what Jamaica chef we have no historical record. But his eyes glowed when he saw at the edge of the table the trenchant sauce ladled into a plate by the hand of Hannah herself.

I saw no fruit in the chutney, but a hot aroma arose from the plate and it promptly wafted across the table and as promptly placed me in a daze.

Errol excavated a spoonful from the plate, opened his mouth and placed the potion upon his tongue. He held it there as if savoring an ambrosia. But I noticed that his color changed, his face reddened, his eyes began to tear and he rose from the table. Here he took another heaping table-spoonful and jammed it between his teeth and against his left cheek, like a chaw of tobacco in the old days. There was a third tablespoon of the East Indian delicacy still left on the plate, and Errol scooped it up and placed it into and against his right cheek. His mouth and throat, his teeth and tonsils were now saturated with mustard, garlic, vinegar and chili—and, so they say, some fruit.

And now he began the Chutney Dervish, or the Chutney Swing or the Chutney Quake. Give it your own title.

His face perspired and his skin became the color of a ripe tomato.

Make no mistake: he was having a wonderful time. This was *taste*.

A steak wouldn't do it, pheasant wouldn't do it, apple pie never. This was a taste that sent you reeling away from the table, holding your face and jaw with both hands, your feet pedaling up and down as if on a bicycle, your whole body in pain and sensation—that was *taste*. That was something to eat, to feed upon.

Chocolate, poof.

Cake, yuks.

Lamb chops, yech.

But something that made him stand on his chair, which he now did, and then threaten to mount the table itself— which frightened me because I was hungry and didn't want to see all that food trampled upon—and screaming in pain, stepping down to the floor again, while he swigged water, vodka and other liquids to soothe his throat and placate his stomach somewhat while he continued to gyrate—that something pleased him.

It pleased him as I have never seen any other person pleased.

It pleasured him because it was both food and sensation at the same time.

It exorcised and exercised him because it was physical experience out of the ordinary and it was aberration, both of which he loved and lived by.

And I want to tell you, ladies and gentlemen (one of his favorite parenthetical remarks), all of us had one helluva great time watching him do the Chutney Dervish.

Dhondi and I were dancing about the big living room of Hannah's place to the music of *South Pacific*. A stereo was going, the record whirling. So were we. Errol was in another room.

When the record came to an end, I started to play it over.

Errol came tearing into the room and with all the sarcasm he could muster when he once in a while said pittttttt-eeeeeeee, he argued, "Do we have to hear *South Pacific* twice in one afternoon?"

Absolutely not. I got to the stereo even before fast Dhondi could and the pleasantry ended.

Later it dawned on me that the New Guinea he had known, tough jungle, bow-and-arrow bedecked aborigines, clap, malaria, the dank waters of the Sepik, the murderous competitions of the gold fields, his trial for murder: it was an altogether different South Pacific than the one dreamed up by the combined genius of Rogers and Hammerstein.

Listening and festering there in the privacy of his room, perhaps moved to thinking back to his days in New Guinea, his bumming times in Australia, his flight from Tasmania, all the realities of his hard early manhood—*South Pacific* must have been to him irritating false rubbish.

While we were at Hannah's a phone call came from Port Antonio. It was his caretaker of Boston House. Errol listened in silence.

"It's burned right to the foundation?" he finally asked.

Apparently it was. He registered no surprise or emotion. "The whole place is down? It is all burned out?"

There was more talk, mostly from the other end. Errol said, "I'll be back there in a few days. I'll come out and look at it."

That was all.

Each of us jumped in with inquiry. What had burned down?

"Boston House."

"All down? Burned right out?"

"Yes, to the stone foundation."

I recalled he had gotten insurance on the place only recently. And how timely it was that this place burned down just when he began building a new home not far away from Boston House. What a coincidence.

A little later when he and I were alone and I commiserated with him about the burning, he chuckled, that deep throaty sardonic laugh when something either mattered or didn't matter. "I burned it down," he said.

"What do you mean?"

"Kerosene, sport. I had a man go out there last night and take care of the whole thing."

"Are you serious?"

"Sure I'm serious." He laughed again, from down in the throat.

To this day I don't know whether he told the truth or not, whether he had his place burned down or whether he merely took the situation that way and tried to claim fun credit for it. Either was possible with him.

Later when we returned to the north of Jamaica we went out to see Boston House. Nothing was left but the stone foundation, four hundred years old. His father's large marine biology library had gone up in the blaze. The pimento wine had either been removed or was boiled to death.

The place looked ghostly: just the stone base and a hollow of ash where the cellar had been.

But the big new house was now going up.

The day came for us to return to Port Antonio. It had been a happy time for Errol.

At night the insects were troublesome. They seemed to get through the screens and morning found them dead on floor, pillow, bedsheet and bureau. I remember that, and I remember the fit of depression over Errol as we took leave.

We were driving back, and when we arrived in a town that Errol knew and stopped in front of a physician's house that Errol also knew, he got out of the front seat and walked through a gate along a concrete pathway to the doctor's door. No more than thirty feet away. The air was clear, the

sunlight strong. No noise, and voices carried. When the
M.D. came to the door Errol did not say hello doctor or
identify himself—I don't think he had to do that—he
merely intoned a word that came out long, very long, like
a lament, and I heard the word in strong phonetic character
sweep back to the road: "M-o-o-o-o-r-r-r-f-e-e-e-e-e-n-n."

I heard the doctor say cryptically, "I have no morphine."

Errol sang once more out of his despond and need.
"M-M-O-O-O-O-R-R-R-R-F-E-E-E-E-E-N-N."

Twice, and the doctor again louder said, "No morphine."

The doctor invited him inside.

He was in there a few minutes.

The doctor gave him Seconal.

For the rest of the ride home he seemed dopey.

He had gone without a shot of the hard stuff ever since
we had been at Hannah's house.

That evening, about eleven o'clock, the Kingston physician and the woman came tearing into the side yard of the
Titchfield—they had received an emergency call from Errol
when he returned—and the doctor, with his medical kit,
went up the stairs hurriedly. He took Errol into the bathroom and gave him his shot.

Errol slept the next day until two o'clock.

I marveled that for one who drank all day—save for occasional intervals of brief abstinence—he rarely showed the
usual signs of heavy drink. Once or twice I had seen him
tipsy enough to be poor of locomotion, but it was rarely
that he needed any steadying or help. If he got into a
moment like that he was inclined to withdraw, to sense he
wasn't behaving right and to get out of sight.

But there was one other symptom that appeared in him from time to time. It was a moment of paranoia that must have been induced by heavy intake. These were mysterious moments that left me baffled at the time.

Once I was seated at the bar of the Titchfield talking to a traveling salesman in from Kingston. He was a chocolate-colored man, amiable, friendly, selling something, I forget what, and he had once met Errol. Now he was talking to me about life on the island of Jamaica.

Suddenly Errol walked straight toward us, came over close, bent down, looked straight at me, then straight at the salesman, and in a threatening way said, "I know you're talking about me. You have no business being together. You had better not be either. Hear?"

We were both upset, the salesman and myself. We hadn't given him a thought, weren't talking about him at all.

But somehow the harsh approach had the effect of separating me from this stranger. I looked at him, he looked at me, and we decided not to talk to each other any further. I walked off. He walked off. We never saw each other again.

I couldn't figure out what had hit Errol, but decided later on that he was deep into vodka, that it was doing something to him and he had made this unexpected suspicious move.

The same thing happened another time. I was in the pool by myself, swimming. I often swam there, sometimes escaping from Errol, from the book, from the scene by ten or fifteen intensive moments of splashing about by myself.

Errol came alongside the pool, knelt down as I swam by and in that same strange manner, almost of abstraction, as if he were talking or acting in a dream, said, "I know your game. You feel if you drown you won't have to work with me. As you've already gathered most of my story, you'll

take the story to the bottom of the pool with you forever.
That's your game, isn't it?" It was said coldly, sternly, ab-
sently. It wasn't one of his jokes. He was deep in his cups
again.

"Whatever you say, Errol," and I moved out of the pool.

There was still a third encounter. The third has lingered
with me, as a haunt of how his intensive drinking did once
in a while manifest itself, not in a man who stumbled or
couldn't speak well, but in an odd statement that made no
sense.

At the dining room table, at lunchtime, there were just
the two of us. He had been drinking heavily since eight
o'clock that morning. He had talked for four hours, the
longest stretch of reminiscence he ever engaged in. Even
there at the table, as he dined lightly on something or
other, his hand went for the glass of vodka more often than
for any of the food. He said, "You've remarked on how
fresh the Jamaica coffee is. I told you it was grown in the
mountains here, four thousand feet above sea level." Looking me straight in the eye and in dead seriousness, he
continued: "Is that any reason for you to have dropped that
arsenic in my cup?"

Then, almost as if he had no idea of what he had said, he
followed up with, "Let's go for a boat ride, Earl."

There weren't many such nonlucid moments. Just those
three that I recall in a year of association with him, watching
him drink case after case of vodka, bottle after bottle of
wine, glass after glass of rum.

Maybe it wasn't a bad record.

Despite his avowals of agnosticism, cynicism, philosophic
futility and the like, there was another side of him that

sometimes reached out into either mysticism, or superstition, or a yearning for a religious crutch to grasp. Sea superstitions hung over him, and one evening at the dinner hour we were standing in the garden in front of the Titchfield looking out along the Navy Island channel that led into the wide-spreading Atlantic. A ribbon sunset covered everything.

Suddenly he shaded his eyes from the still strong sun that glared out of wreaths of violet, purple, scarlet and magenta. I thought I saw him shudder.

"My God . . ." he said. He leaned forward to stare harder at the horizon toward a spot where the ocean became an estuary that led inward to the hotel resort. He put his legs apart as though to better grip the green earth.

"God . . ." he repeated, as if in unbelief.

I looked at him and out there beyond—to nothing.

"The Duppy Ship!" he exclaimed loudly.

I saw no ship.

"The Duppy Ship!"

"Duppy" is a Jamaica term for ghost. He was seeing a ghost ship.

"No one's on it," he murmured. "It's not being manned."

I knew he was a mariner, full of sea lore.

"The sails are red." His head turned slightly as if he followed the course of a moving ship.

I saw the red sunset, nothing else. I stared hard, tried to see what he saw.

Three Jamaicans came to his side, having heard him scream, "Duppy Ship!" They had been at the bar having drinks, but they knew the great Flynn was not like other men. They believed in duppies and he was seeing at long

last the Duppy Ship he had long wanted to see—maybe it
was there.

They took the situation seriously. They palmed their
foreheads and looked down the channel.

"See what I see?" Errol turned to them.

Goddamit, they said they did!

"Yep, dem Duppy Ship!"

All three screamed, "Dem Duppy Ship! Mista Fleen bring-
en in dem Duppy Ship!"

Errol turned to me as if it were proved. "You see?"

I saw nothing but the velvet-covered channel of water,
the darkening sky out beyond, the purple Atlantic. I wished
I could see something; I might be less shook up. Why the
hell were these Jamaicans yelling about the Duppy Ship and
claiming they saw it too?

Later I learned that voodoo is a deep streak in Jamaica
and the claim of seeing ghosts is readily believed by a great
many. No one questions ghosts. Ghosts will walk through
walls.

Now they were hailing the Duppy Ship along with Flynn
—or perhaps expecting to get paid for confirming what he
saw.

Errol's eyes appeared to follow the slow motion of the
empty boat toward us, with no one aboard alive or dead or
sailing it.

Errol turned, shaken, and staggered back to the hotel
and up to his room.

One of the Jamaicans turned to me, "You see dem?"

I shook my head.

Errol had been drinking heavily all day.

Still, I was unsteadied. Maybe he was capable of seeing
things I couldn't see.

At night the whole region was ghostly with high hills, waving palms that fanned in the moonlight, sounds of dogs barking all over, hooting of owls, night sounds of birds that lived at night.

I couldn't sleep.

Duppy Ship. Goddam.

A man, young and well dressed, came to see him at the hotel. There had been a prior phone talk. The caller said he had a big deal to offer Errol, would he be interested?

Errol rarely or never turned down a prospective money-making operation: it could be real estate, a film, a play, the purchase of a chicken yard, he would listen. "Come by," Errol said. "Two o'clock."

Errol turned to me and said, "Earl, sit at the table with me when this guy shows. Let's see what he has to offer."

At two o'clock the call came from the desk. "Mr. Sartorub is here."

We went down. Sartorub recognized Errol and Errol introduced me: "My lawyer. I like to have him sit in on deals." I was surprised to find myself cast in this new role. Naturally I kept quiet.

Mr. Sartorub outlined a film based on the famous White Witch of Rose Hall that appears to be the classic story of the island of Jamaica. Involved is murder, a haunted house, voodoo, wealth—all the clichés. The story is located in Jamaica and the original event happened there a long time ago.

"I'm interested in that," said Errol. "Always have been. Think I can get my Hollywood friends to do it if we have a screenplay, some Jamaica money and the right woman to play the White Witch."

Mr. Sartorub visibly illumined. It looked like everything was going smoothly.

"This film has to be financed," he said, "and I think I can raise some Jamaica money for this, but I'd hope you can participate in the financing or get your Hollywood connections to take over on that."

Errol gave me the faintest side glance as much as to say, "This is what I want you to watch."

"We'd share in this, then," Errol surmised, "I to put up a portion of this and you to be able to put up a portion. Perhaps my friends in Los Angeles to pitch in too. Right?"

"That's the idea."

"You understand," Errol said, "that's a film that would cost millions to make, maybe three or four. All of Jamaica is involved: its wealth, its color problems, its English tradition and its African background."

"I realize it. That's why I think it would make a great film."

Errol whipped a checkbook out of his pocket. He asked me for a pen. He said to Sartorub, "I can write a check for two million. What can you do?"

Mr. Sartorub blanched. He pulled back in his chair. He didn't expect this was the time when he would have to put up or shut up, or just appear to be promoting something, "scratching," as the media industry put it.

"Ah, era . . . a uh . . . emmm . . . oh aa . . ." The sounds went on longer than that.

Errol put the checkbook back in his pocket.

"Get in touch with me when you get your half together," Errol said, rising.

He turned to me, "Ready for that swim?"

•   •   •

Errol often said that what took him anywhere and every-where in the world, and what was his virtue and his defect, was his curiosity. I found this to be true.

He was curious about an insect, the look of the sky, the hole in the trunk of a tree. He would even halt whatever he was doing to take an interest in something that was much less interesting.

As we stood by a fence a few dozen yards away from the hotel, a young black man went by with a paper bag under his arm. The fellow was about forty yards distant. Errol beckoned him: a gesture of his index finger, and the man halted but did not come to us.

Errol left me and walked toward the passerby. The young man started moving toward him. They met halfway.

Errol said, "Man, what you got in bag? Let me see."

The fellow held the bag open while Errol peeked inside. I don't know what he saw in there but it couldn't have been anything other than some groceries: perhaps a breadfruit, a few bananas, nothing more.

His curiosity was satisfied.

His sister Rosemary, from Washington, D.C., had been with us for several days. She was a pretty, well-built woman in her late thirties, not a physical reminder of Errol facially, but handsome, healthy looking, sturdy, Irish, wholesome and feminine. She was amiable, humorous, soft-voiced and her brother's admirer.

Rosemary was a total opposite to her brother, with none of Errol's chameleon and unpredictable character. She was anonymous, retiring, obscure, all of which was such a con-trast to the ever-present and impacting Errol. Her tinkly laughter, her right comments, a certain correctness about her is what chiefly I remember.

Marelle and Professor Flynn had certainly done other things with her than with her famous brother.

I remembered only one story Errol told of her: that once, when he had become famous, in the late 1930s, Rosemary had arrived in New York and he had flown in to see her. They had gone about for a few days, to the Stork, to other clubs, and Errol tried to bridge the age gap of ten years that was between them. She was nineteen or twenty, inexperienced, new to the world, as it were, and he had by now riveted into his character his spectacular, congealed past. After a few days he found an attractive young lady at the Stork, ran away from Rosemary and began a new romance.

It must be, I decided, that they rarely saw each other, but now they were together again.

The period of the visit of Errol's sister may have been about a week and a half. The recollection of her presence is shadowy, only because this lovely woman was of such a retiring disposition: nothing at all like her energetic and effervescent brother. I recollect her laughter, her being about the hotel, the swimming pool, alongside of us on rides about the region, and I remember mostly her last two days in Jamaica.

Errol was feeling poorly and decided to go into Kingston Hospital for a day or so. The attack of ptomaine or whatever it was that had been produced in him by the raw meat and egg yolk left him weak and worried. Time to get a liver, heart and overall checkup.

All of us motored across the island. The Jamaica driver, Errol, Dhondi and myself were in one car. Rosemary was in another. We had been driving for a time when Errol decided to lift the boredom. He slid into one of his not infrequent macho or prank moods. A small bit of sadism, or sport, as he might put it himself, sufficient to liven a dull auto trip.

Errol was talking about his vasectomy. He was thinking of having the vasectomy undone (if that was possible at the time; I didn't know it was). He kept telling Dhondi, "Now, the night before the surgery I have to go to bed with the nurse. The nurse has to go to bed with me and there are certain things the nurse does that prepare me for the surgeon."

He must have told her that, deadpan, scores of times before we set out. This time he insisted on involving me in his plan. He nudged me demanding that I stick with him on this one.

As the chauffeur-driven car swerved around the curves he reminded her of what must happen with the nurse. His face was grimly serious, as if he regretted the procedure.

It must be borne in mind that this was the classic Errol Flynn at work. No one who ever met him and spent a few hours with him will doubt this story.

It's no strain on my memory to recall it at all.

This time, as the shadow of a wink passed from him to me, he made that matter-of-fact statement that was really a taunt, as he probed her face to get a reaction. "You understand I have to do this?"

"Aw goddamit," she screamed, and it seemed she was really convinced, "I know you gotta go to bed with the bitch nurse. Lemme alone!"

While Errol was in the hospital getting X-rayed, plumbed, poked and measured, Rosemary, Dhondi and myself were at a motel on the outskirts of the city.

Errol came out of the hospital, spent a day or so at the motel recouping before we were to motor back to Port Antonio. The doctors told him it was mysterious how and why he was alive: his liver was shot, there was more alcohol in his veins than blood. Other such details.

But the recovery sense in him was at work. In a few hours, after pills and a resumption of drinks, he was sitting up, then moving around, then laughing from his throat and belly and being himself again. Overnight he was the same figure we all knew.

Back at the Titchfield Rosemary prepared to return to the States. After she left, Errol made a decision about Dhondi.

"You've got to go back to the States. You are going back right now."

Dhondi looked terror-stricken. "Why?"

"You have to go back. You must get this thing straightened out with your parents."

"Aw . . ."

"No aw-w-w-w about it. You have to get straight with your father."

Dhondi's father was outraged that his daughter had taken up with Errol. There was no way in the world Dhondi could straighten out anything with him. Her mother went along with the romance. She even thought it a great thing; she had been a stage mother to Dhondi since the girl was a baby, and figured that was life and Hollywood.

They fought bitterly. Errol raised his voice as if he were going offstage after slaying four Shakespearean court villains. Dhondi raised her voice in what was going to be a losing battle. I was embarrassed, sorry to be a witness.

She bawled like a little girl, which she was. She knew damned well he would be cavorting with the dames who came around the hotel. She had been with him steadily for a couple of years and she felt endangered. Anything could happen. He could take up with someone else.

Good as my memory is I can't recall the dialogue, because it wasn't dialogue. It was hollering and weeping.

Now he meant to bring it to an end—for a time anyway. He had other designs for the period he would remain in Jamaica before returning to New York.

Dhondi flew out.

Evening in the Jamaica moonlight.

We were sitting in a ring on the grass about thirty yards behind the pool and beneath a palm. Young black men and black women were dancing, and the yellow of the moon refracted on their dark skins. Someone was passing about a stub of ganja. Each one took a puff, passed it to the next person. You could go to jail for twenty years in Jamaica if you were caught with a bit of that on you. But that night everybody had a puff, some had two or three, some had a whole cigarette of it to themselves. I hadn't touched the stuff in twenty-five years and it had never meant much to me: never cared for its sweet, sickening odor. But that night I had my puff, danced with a Jamaica girl calypsoing and limboing opposite me, and the black musicians were strumming their instruments and singing Jamaica songs about the Yankee dollah and running Venezuela and the like.

Errol pranced about wearing only a pair of shorts, a towering figure larger than all others, doing the Jamaica steps, smoking his bit of pot, going over occasionally for a sip of vodka from the glass resting on the pool edge.

The girls flocked about Errol. Once he went off into the woods for about twenty minutes. Then the drummers and guitarists played for me, for themselves, for the people sitting around that circle.

It went on like this for several hours, dalliance under the Jamaica moon, a bit of lawbreaking, a bit of rum and fun.

Above the trees the moon laughed in a silver sky, approving the song and dance and calypso time around the hotel.

When the party broke up at midnight Errol suggested, "Let's go into town."

He told the night receptionist, "Send for a cab."

He turned to me, his face alight. "I am going to take you somewhere," he said.

"Good!"

"A house of special integrity," he said.

Where the hell had I heard that before? A house of special integrity!

Only a few weeks before he had told me of his first meeting with John Barrymore in Hollywood at a time when Errol hadn't even made a picture yet and Barrymore was the famed Profile. Barrymore, intoxicated, had gotten into a talk with Errol on a studio set. Errol had mentioned the Far East and Barrymore was delighted: he recalled a house of special integrity in Kuala Lumpur, in fact a whorehouse of special integrity.

Moreover, I recollected that Errol several times had used "house of special integrity," and it always meant a whorehouse.

A few days before Doc Lawrence had told me that the biggest complaint in all Jamaica was venereal. "If one is promiscuous around here you can't escape it. It's general. My biggest problem."

Soon we heard the cab roll up to the hotel. I found myself following Errol down the staircase, wondering just how I would handle the situation.

As we got into the back seat Errol bent forward and told the driver, "Edward, take us to the Golden Hallway."

"Golden Hallway, Meester Fleen?"

"Yes, that house of very special integrity."

The cabbie didn't push the accelerator.

"You sure you wantem dem Golden Hallway?"

"That's what I said."

Edward looked at me and I must have looked unhappy. It was one of the few real moments of unhappiness since I got to Jamaica. Most of it had been fun. Now I kept hearing Doc Lawrence's comment on the social condition thereabouts.

"Ah, Meester Fleen, you don't wanten dem go Golden Hallway. It no good there. Nobody get away good there. Nobody!"

Here the cab driver was echoing the local medical opinion.

Errol looked abashed. I didn't know how he figured to get around the venereal prospect.

"Maybe we shouldn't, Errol," I suggested. "Maybe this is the smartest cab driver in the Caribbean."

Errol let out one of his hearty throaty laughs. Crazy bastard. Either he wasn't afraid of getting the Pearl of Great Price again, or he didn't care whether he involved me or not, or he had had too much vodka, or he was Errol Flynn.

"Take us down into town anyway," Errol said.

We drove a few hundred yards and got out. We walked the streets. "I want to show you the Golden Hallway—just the outside of it."

"Okay with me," I said. "A look. But really, Errol . . ."

"You're no Bud Ernst," he said, with that throaty laugh. Bud had been his pal at houses of integrity for twenty years.

"And you're no Freddie McEvoy."

McEvoy and he had done the bit at houses of integrity in Australia.

"And no Barrymore . . ."

"Never been to Kuala Lumpur," I admitted. "Besides, I want to write that book of yours. What the hell are you trying to do to me?"

"Sometimes," Errol murmured, "I don't understand my-self."

The sun was just coming up, but very low: you could see the light in the sky, but not the curve of the orb. We were headed back to the hotel.

As you go through the streets of Port Antonio at dawn the town looks like an old English village: its architecture, its layout. The vicious little dogs of Jamaica bark and howl steadily.

It was from the howling of these mongrel dogs that I learned that all over the world they communicate. They have a language, they understand one another when they bark. You and I don't know what they are saying, but one dog knows just what sentiment and thought and point the other is making.

The noisy dogs of Jamaica talk all night long to one another, howl across the town to their friends who howl back. You cannot sleep in that town. The dogs' symphony goes on, beginning at eight or nine o'clock in the evening and not dying out until the roosters start at sunrise. It is a vicious communication in which they are speaking ill of their lives in Jamaica, of their masters, of the cyclonic storms, the heat and the insects that bite them and make them scratch and bleed day and night.

They are irritable canines about a foot-and-a-half long and a foot or so high. You can't see their nasty hair-covered faces. They are pompous wretches who zealously guard the properties on which they live.

They are obstreperous creatures. Don't get near them. They'll take a bite out of you as big as a filet mignon. It's happened.

I hated the mutts and so did Errol, much as he loved dogs generally.

At this hour we were passing various properties and the dogs barked at us and said, "Go on, carousers, go home."

We went lightly through the streets, both of us tipsy, using the fences to hold ourselves up.

At last we came near a house where the dog with the loudest bark, the worst disposition and everything else unpleasant that a dog can be was trying hard to scramble up over his wire fence to get out and take two filet mignons, Errol's and mine.

"Listen to that loud-mouthed cur," I said to Errol.

Errol could hardly hear me for the noise the wretch was making. The dog was all mouth, throat and jaw, and he was letting his pals on the other side of town know that he was doing his sentinel duty properly and that detestable human wretches were threatening something that he thought belonged to him or his master.

Errol picked up a rock. A damned good rock. The rock fitted Errol's large fist. It must have weighed 2½ pounds.

"What are you going to do?"

He didn't answer. I didn't have to ask.

He stealthily approached the fence. That fence wasn't so high. The dog had the mobility of his entire yard and he was pawing his way up over the interstices of the fence to get outside. He just wanted to bite—anybody, anything.

And the poor sonofabitch picked on Errol Flynn. Fool dog.

Errol came close to the fence, his hand held high, the rock clutched there. The dog had his head up over the fence and he knew something was wrong: this two-legged thing was supposed to run, to hurry by. Instead, he was advancing with something in his hand overhead.

I stepped in close. I had no fear. The swashbuckler was going to save me and Samarkand and Kuala Lumpur and Port Antonio all in one.

In the increasing light I saw a gleam in Errol's small eyes. The night would not be wasted.

The dog could have leaped a couple of feet and caught Errol's belly, but instead Errol came down with all his might on the animal's head with that rock, enough of a blow to kill the dog. The mongrel let out a terrible screech and collapsed to the ground.

Errol and I ran like hell for the hotel.

Candidly, I felt good about it. Don't ask me why. I was with Errol and against the dog.

How could a man who loved dogs as Errol did, who called them "small companions," who had had dogs at his side in Tasmania, New Guinea, Australia, Hollywood, on the *Zaca*—how could a dog lover like that crack down on this cur's head in that fashion?

It was the simple principle of contradiction that inhered in him as solidly as a principle in physics. He contained the thesis and the antithesis of living: Hegel would have loved him.

Maybe that two-pound rock was the synthesis.

After our talks Errol often said, almost as a daily ritual, "Let's face it, you and I are alike."

Him and me alike?

At first I didn't know what he meant. His career had been totally different. Physically we were as unalike as two people from the ends of the earth, which we were: he from Tasmania and the culture of "lands down under" and I a central New Yorker; he a consumer of alcohol, drugs and an incessant smoker, I a coffee hound. In large tastes and in small tastes it seemed to me that we differed. And we looked so unalike as we walked together, he large, looming, handsome, and I a middle-sized chap.

But there the dissimilarities ended, and at that point we did become very much alike: we were very much alike in outlook, feelings and attitudes toward people and the world. We shared a nonreligious view, in the sense of the church, possessed an identity of viewpoint as to man in the cosmos and the cosmos in man. That is much to have in common with anyone. It is like sharing a religion or a faith with another—which can be a great bond. He was critical of and indifferent to the organized church, so was I.

He was in the arts and so was I. We shared similar tastes in literature. I had read what he had read. I was deep into the English tradition of letters, so was he. He knew the writers and poets of the West, so, I felt, did I. He could quote a stanza from Wordsworth or Shelley, so could I. He could sing and dance and tell stories and entertain and be diverting, and I was usually regarded as "a very funny guy."

I provided him with laughs and he provided me with laughs. He was a raconteur and so was I.

This kind of accord went on between us all the time. It was much in common.

He held a great curiosity about man, nature, animals, the physical biosphere, and so did I. As we autoed about Jamaica we shared the marvels of that jungle country. He liked to swim, so did I.

He could work hard, so could I.

That is what he meant by himself and me being alike.

We shared the same ambivalence about the world of politics and the nature of man. We shared Darwinian views about the human specie. He agreed with me when I said man had emerged as the most intense predator in the history of the earth's creation: *vis-à-vis,* what he had done to the biosphere, taking it into his maw and gobbling it up as no other animal had done. He feared nuclear annihilation of the globe, so did I. He mistrusted politicians of any and all ilk, so did I.

So we were very much alike. Being alike does not mean being physically alike. If we weren't mental twins, we had at least reached many similar conclusions, and this was much to have in common with one whose autobiography you are engaged with. I knew how to question him and he had answers for many of those questions.

I knew what troubled me about life and he knew what troubled him.

Even so, the large verities escaped him, as they had escaped me, and as they have escaped all the philosophers I have ever heard of or whose works I have dipped into.

He had glimpses, I had glimpses: almost nothing more.

It is not given to man to know much of the larger world

about us and perhaps not even of those small worlds in ourselves which we call cells.

Seen in this light I felt that Errol was a macrocosm of the "daily man." He might be an Everyman, a little like each of us, with something of all of us inside himself. To deal with him fully might be to deal with each of us in some large part. Moreover, he was verbal. He could express himself. He was a reader. Right there in all that work, as he made love, worked on his life story, swam and sailed daily, drank, gave orders to the help, met with visitors, and sallied back and forth to the bar and to the dining area for his meals, he found time to read.

The man had a maddening desire to know what life was all about and whether it had meaning. His quest to find understanding drove him through the world's wastes. His need to be able to formulate words, definitions, summaries of what the act of living might mean tore at him as a shark tears at its prey. He couldn't find it.

In fact, it was that quest which tore him apart.

I think Errol was trying to make a point but didn't formulate it correctly. In terms of lifestyles, the way we lived, his habits versus my habits, his daily regimen versus mine, we were as far apart as two planets. What he was saying was that I complemented him in a certain way. He seemed surprised at my faculty for probing him, as sometimes I explained him to himself.

I think the chronicler's way of questioning him did him some good, provided a certain therapy or catharsis.

He had once contemplated going to a psychiatrist—that was in Spain in the early 1950s, when he was in great doubt about his life, loss of living interest and loss of Hollywood position. But he never went through with it.

Now I was probing him, going way back to open him up, tossing in experiences of my own that were comparable to his own doubts, to his own findings about people. It was this accord that he dubbed a psychological similarity.

The deep exchange made him think we were alike, and he meant it. But it wasn't exactly true. Perhaps I utter this in regret, I don't know: but I was no playboy, no actor, no barroom brawler, no mariner, no skin diver, no public character, no ten other things. So where the hell were we alike? Where were my three wives, my drugs, movies, copra plantation, my seventy-two mistresses, my two hundred and eighty visits to whorehouses?

Damifino.

We were far along with his story. He had told of his escape from the Australian orbit, his long trek across the globe, over seven seas to London, his apprenticeship in the Northampton Theater, being tagged to go to Hollywood, the more than fifty pictures that followed, the procession of females, the *bouleversing* effect upon him of the rape case: the marriages to Lili Damita, Nora Eddington and Patrice Wymore, the divorces, the costs, the strange unwanted reputation he had acquired of being "in like Flynn," when he hoped to be noted primarily as a dramatic actor. He had poked at the lifetime war with his mother.

He halted once to marvel how through all he had lived he was intact physically, still having all his limbs, all his senses, not quite understanding how this could be.

I continued to probe his questioning nature. "What's your greatest fear?" I asked.

"Castration," he promptly replied.

"Is it an active fear? Something you think about?"

"I certainly do. Take those things away from me and what . . ."

". . . have you got?" I completed.

"Yes, what?" He went on, "I've lived for, with and by my balls. Any guy that's remiss in that quarter might as well be out of the picture."

He looked me in the eye. "You realize what it might be like to go around a eunuch—with that portion of you gone? Know any reason to be alive if you have an accident like that?"

"Did you ever come close to it?"

"I did. That slash I got in India when I was on my way to England with Koets. That little East Indian with the shiv knew how to tangle with a big fellow like me. He snuck down like he was going under a fence, brought his knife up and went for my balls and whang, and fortunately just ripped up my crotch. . . . Take a look."

He lowered his jeans. There on one side was a scar eight or ten inches long—like an overlong appendicitis scar— from his scrotum straight up to his navel. He had barely lived through it and had been hospitalized for a couple of weeks.

"A dreadful prospect," he murmured, as if thinking backward.

I ventured, "Do you think that close shave had any effect on your subsequent sex activity?"

"I wouldn't be surprised. I learned to value my balls so much that possibly I decided to make continual use of them —in the event some small man might one day succeed where this one almost did. Anyway, ever since then I've lived in dread of that one thing—being deballed."

He had one afterthought, and it emerged reflectively. "You can be sure of one thing in this world. Lightning *will* strike twice in the same place."

"Do you have any regrets about anything?"
He was prompt with his answer. "Yes, one deep regret."
"What?"
"That I never learned to play the piano."
As they say in the cliché factory, you could have knocked me over with a feather or an *E* note.

I was stunned. I had expected something profound, high level, maybe something emotional, perhaps a regret he wasn't prime minister of England.

Yet I believe he told the whole truth. What it means to me is that he was a committed entertainer, that he knew the main meaning of his life spelled entertainment, that that was his creative symbolism. And had he been able to play the piano—he could sing pretty well—his repertoire of gifts would have been complete.

I then thought it was a superficial regret but have since changed my mind.

There was one area where he felt uncomfortable. It was his part—or nonpart—in World War II.

Quite probably Errol was the classic "man without a country." Once having quit Tasmania he never had any desire to return there: no sentimentality for the scenes of his childhood. And just about the same reaction to the whole world of "the lands down under." The great effort of his life had been to escape Australia, New Guinea and the rest of that region.

After making it in the West he was, when World War II

broke out, probably the most famous and successful actor in the United States, perhaps in the whole English-speaking world. He had zoomed to the top as if shot from a guided or misguided missile.

Being classified 4-F, having that upheaving rape case experience, he felt alienated. He was willing to have some use made of him by the armed forces in checking out the Sepik River, he told me, in case New Guinea should become a theater of the war. He would be first-rate useful at that, he said, but the government made no such use of him, only wanted him to entertain the soldiers.

Talking to me that morning in his quarters at the Titchfield, muttering about his nonparticipation in the war, when other actors had joined the services, he seemed in low gear, half apologetic about it all.

Though he had taken out American citizenship in 1942, he had, I believe, no real feeling of relationship to the United States scene. He would find his home, his milieu, his natural habitat in 1947 when the *Zaca,* after a storm, drifted into the harbor of Kingston, Jamaica.

He made several highly praised war pictures and he had the pants kidded off him for winning the war in the movies —somewhat single-handed—while not actually shouldering a rifle in the real conflict.

Later I wondered whether there was a hidden or even a clear-cut connection between Errol's nonparticipation in the service and the decision of some Los Angeles second-rate politicos, jealous of his fame and economic success, to throw the book at him then and there, during the war, and let him have that statutory rape charge. He was a very vulnerable figure for no-talent, no-future politicians.

It can be understandable too that government officials

who tossed a false criminal charge at him immediately after he was granted citizenship would not necessarily win great fealty from him.

We were moving idly alongside the swimming pool. He seemed ready to speak of something, eyed me, turned his head thoughtfully, ventured, "There's something I've been thinking of. . . ."

He slowed as a faraway look slipped over his bronzed face. "I don't think I . . . we . . . maybe it shouldn't be told."

He had so far concealed nothing.

"What is it, Errol? Spill it. Get it off your chest. Think of me as your shrink. We may or may not use it. Spill it anyway."

"No, no. I can't." He stood still. I stopped with him.

"Errol, this is a helluva thing. You haven't held back anything so far."

He looked at me several times with what the showbiz trade calls double takes. He murmured, "I wonder if . . ."

My ears perked. It was as if this were an effort at confession.

"I am wondering whether . . ." he hesitated. "No, I can't . . . I just can't."

I was totally interested. "Aw, come on, Errol, get it off your chest."

"It was . . ." he started. Then he shook his head vigorously. Same troubled look, brow furrowed. "No, I better not."

He studied my reaction. Should I prompt him? Leave him to reveal of his own accord? A problem.

He halted again. I thought he would talk now. What could it possibly be that he hesitated about? He had told me how in self-defense he had shot a native in New Guinea, been tried for murder: no hesitation there. He had leaped to confess his triumphs over females, his deviltry in finance, a bastard when he fought with Hollywood bastards, bragged of whaffing people and getting whaffed himself, confessed to stealing, being part of the Woolamaloo gang: everything.

"C'mon, Errol," I urged. "Don't pull punches now."

"No. I absolutely can't." He waved his hands, as if to say, that's finished: no tell.

I prompted him no further, but I remained plagued. What the hell had he done that was worse than killing someone? What could anyone do worse than that? If anyone could do worse, he was probably the guy.

Curiosity about what he hesitated to disclose poked at me. "Errol," I said, "autobiography to succeed and be great has to be revelatory. Shoot the works. The reader forgives candor no matter how revealing it may be. The reader is with you if you are telling a great story."

He was silent, still shaking his head. "No . . . it's too much. I won't. I can't tell it."

Was this one of his tricks to arouse suspense and curiosity in me, as much as to say: I have already told you Aladdin wonders about a strange youthtime, but I will not tell this last thing, this ultra experience?

The conclusion I console myself with is that he was an actor, at all times the actor . . . and that this was an act, one of his pranks. I believe he couldn't and didn't keep a thing to himself, but he had sprung this lure on me to kid me deeply and amuse himself.

The hurricane season was on in the Caribbean. Everybody was restive except Errol. A hurricane was easy for him; it was his element. He was calm, sipping rather a bit more vodka and tonic than usual, happily consuming cigarettes, pacing about, watching the sky as if it were a show. I noted in him a keen awareness of the weather, as if the cyclone in his own nature rose to meet the external one that moved toward us. He glanced at the darkening sky as one who has seen this before. He went about with an inward readiness for disaster, probably the prime mood of his whole existence.

I was fretful, had never seen a hurricane before or been in one. Out there, in and over the Atlantic, it looked whirling and dark; there was a big blotch at the center. He said that was "the eye" and if it hit us, he added, forget about the book.

The eye seemed to be coming straight at us, slowly, steadily, directly into the North Shore of Jamaica.

"It might veer," he said. "Hurricanes have funny minds. Nobody knows what makes them turn this way or that. It may wind up hitting New York."

About the hotel everything was flapping. Winds tore up the curtains. Rain was coming down in a tearful way but not really crying yet. They had taken in the chairs and tables from the porch.

The water in the swimming pool churned.

There was no fun spirit anywhere. The blacks looked worried. They were sitting or standing about, or they had gone back to their families in their huts.

For many days we did little work. It was too noisy as the wind hit the blinds, shuddered the hotel. But I had a chance to note Errol's endless motions, to see how he dealt with people, followed up plans on his new house, talked with his lawyers and with business people. Deals. He was always interested in a deal, and most of the business people who came to this town wound up at the Titchfield bar.

If the eye of the big wind hit, hundreds of lives would be lost, the small huts would be blown down, Port Antonio would be a shambles. The Titchfield might not be left standing.

Errol said, "I've a key to a stone door underneath that pool. When I owned this hotel I had a hurricane cellar built below the pool. The pool has a strong cement base. It will act as a ceiling for us if the wind hits. There's several hundred square feet of space underneath that can hold a half dozen of us for about ten hours."

"Is there any air down there?"

"Damned little. That was the only thing we couldn't figure out. If we open the door we can let air get in for a while, then we'll have to close the door when the strike comes and hope there's enough air in the place to keep us alive for a few hours."

We were at the bar having that talk; then, in the midst of it, he quietly disappeared.

For half an hour I stayed there and watched the sky. I was nervous, nothing to do but smoke cigarettes, sip rum, exchange a word or two with other drinkers.

I wondered where Errol was and what he might be doing.

Not that I didn't have an idea.

Eddy, who functioned as Errol's procurer of black girls, had come by the bar with a girl about the time Errol went off to his room. The young woman was about twenty, not very pretty but built solidly and wearing the poor cotton clothes that many Jamaican girls wore.

Eddy delivered the young lady to Errol.

In about half an hour Errol returned to the bar, and together we watched the arduous performance of the hurricane again. He ventured the speculation that the big wind would probably turn elsewhere. "Know what I was doing?" he asked.

I looked at him quizzically. He said, "Earl, the finest go in the world is when there is a big wind on. When you keep time to the sound of those blasts hitting the window, when the rain is a roar in your ears, it's exciting. You don't get a chance for a bout like that more than once a year."

I tried for a humble understatement. "I'm very happy that this particular hurricane hasn't been a total loss for just everybody in the Caribbean this time around."

There was something I didn't understand. "Errol," I asked, "when you have a female around don't you require some personality, some mentality in the creature, something to talk about, something in common, ideas, an intellectual accord? You get what I mean? You know you're quite a mental fellow."

"I missed the mental stimulation when I was younger," he answered. "But from the time I began to have women, shall we say, on the assembly-line basis, I discovered that the only thing you need, want or should have is the absolutely physical. Simply the physical. No mind at all. A woman's mind will get in the way."

"Really?"

"For me . . . I am speaking of myself. I don't speak for male humankind. I am speaking for what I've discovered or what I need: the body, the face, the physical motion, the voice, the femaleness, the female presence . . . totally that, nothing else. That's the best. There's no possessiveness in that."

I watched him closely.

"I'm serious," he said. "That's my view and feeling. Just the elementary physical female. Nothing more than that. When you get hold of that—hang on to it, for a short while."

I must have looked perplexed. He continued, "The less you know about your partner the better. The surprise, the unexpected, the feeling that here, of a sudden, is a new and unknown quantity—and you're experiencing it. That's the thing. That's where the thrill is. That's why I like buying them, having them—and going on to another next time around."

This is the same chap who, remember, said he entered a whorehouse with the same interest as he did the British Museum or the Metropolitan—in the same spirit of curiosity.

He must have meant it.

For myself, I who knew the fellow say simply, with a shrug of my shoulders, "Judge not, that ye be not judged."

The only other thing I can think of that might be observed was the point of independence, self-realization and self-penetration uttered by him.

There is a historical passage of the Irish poet W. B. Yeats, who may have been speaking of Errol Flynn when he described the guts it might take to really enter into one's own nature, as the swashbuckler did. Said Yeats:

"Why should we honor those that die upon the field of battle, a man may show as reckless a courage in entering into the abyss of himself."

I think Yeats would have understood Errol.

Not long afterward the eye of the big wind turned elsewhere.

The rain came, and it rained badly for several hours.

We gathered more intimately about the bar. Life began again. It was the second hurricane threat we were to have in three weeks.

"There'll be another one or two," Errol said. "This is the season. I'm used to them. We had them all the time around New Guinea. Guess I can't live without them."

I said, "Errol, if there was anything in nature I'd liken your life to, it would be a wild hurricane that was hit in the eye by life."

"Write it like that," he said.

He felt livened. "Shall we work, sport?"

Back at his quarters, with the wind and rain lessening, I ventured once more deeply into his days.

It was evening. He snapped on a light. He went to a suitcase and drew out a minute globule, about five inches high and only a couple of inches in width.

I thought of it as a bit of metal blob, or if not metal then some composition of clay or stone. He said, "Amphora."

I stared at it. It was a vase, minute, with two handles on each side, a belly like an egg and a tight neck like a swan's, with an orifice at the top. I could see neither practical nor ornamental use for it. It had a surface like a marble egg-shell, little dots over it.

He explained that he had brought it up from the bottom of the sea off the Spanish island of Ibiza. It dated, he said, back to about 350 B.C. It seemed to please him more than any ecstasy he might have gotten from any woman, but in an altogether different way.

It thrilled the "scientist" and artist in him. It exhilarated that portion of him which was descended from his philosophic and scientist father: that father in whom he took such pride and yet from whom he differed in so many respects.

He was aware of the civilizations below the sea, below land; aware of how time, winds and quakes have uprooted soils, covered cities.

How little, he wondered, can man tell about the past from archaeology. How little from a piece of metal or gold or a trinket that hung about some woman's neck, or from this amphora two thousand years old?

Or maybe we can tell a lot, he surmised. Maybe we can tell that things aren't much different today.

Maybe the baubles that the women wore in the Bible they still wear. Maybe the necklaces, anklets, rings in the noses and ears and toes are all the same now as once in the Garden of Eden, or along the Nile, or the Yangtse, or with the native citizens along the Missouri ten thousand years ago.

Maybe, he thought, it doesn't change.

This is what that amphora meant to him.

He had retrieved it and he felt like an archaeologist touching upon the past, bridging two thousand years.

Errol had gone below water many times in search of sunken galleys, and this once at least he had come near a ravaged hulk that might have been such. He had rummaged through the debris and come up with the amphora.

The word came from him like music.

I was at all times aware of what Errol Flynn stood for in society. He stood for much. I would try to visualize the Herculean labors he had performed in his fifty-four films (his last film, the fifty-fifth, *Cuban Rebel Girls*, was made later). I saw lines of people queued up before theater marquees waiting to get in to see him dash bravely through some romance or adventure. I visualized people in the streets holding a newspaper in their hands and gazing with amusement possibly at some banner headline, FLYNN WINS $15,000 FROM CONFIDENTIAL. (At one time there had been a scandal magazine whose offerings of inside information upset most of the Hollywood celebrities, their alleged private lives being exposed, and much of the so-called exposure a likely invention. Errol had fought back, sued for some large sum, collected a small one. But he was tired of being portrayed as an incessant roué. He didn't mind being "guilty" of the things he had done, but disliked false accusations). In his room, tossed carelessly on a bureau, were two books he had done when younger, *Beam Ends,* the story of a 3,000-mile sailboat trip he and some companions took from Australia to New Guinea, and *Showdown,* a novel based on his New Guinea experiences. A few miles away was a $2 million copra acreage—and he had once been penniless. The experience of being about him was therefore a curious and compelling one.

From time to time, though, he denigrated himself. He called his lifestyle "fatuous" and, worst of all, downgraded his enormous film career. We were seated now about a round table on the plaza of the swimming pool, and there, sitting before me, he flayed himself in tones of dejection. "I've made six or seven good films," he opined, "the others not so good."

I was surprised at that self-judgment.

He went on, "I was doing okay, I think, till they threw that rape rap at me. Then when I lost my feeling for living I also lost the necessary feeling you have to have to put on your best performance. I became don't care about it all. I made the pictures that the studios wanted me to make, Westerns, mediocre vehicles. I walked through them and reviewers remarked that I walked through them. I had lost my chance to become a Barrymore. They had me typed and stereotyped, but I had two families by then, I needed money."

He was faltering, apologizing, regretting, and it was painful to hear. I felt his self-criticism was unfair and untrue. But listening, I realized that the period from 1950 to the present was most painful to him. His pulling power with Warner Studios had waned. I gathered that his film *Don Juan*, made in 1948, had not been a moneymaker for Warner Brothers and that the studio had decided not to invest heavily in any of his future productions.

In 1952 he broke with Jack Warner and went to Europe to make films. He returned to a few costume-type vehicles; he lost much money on a proposed film, *William Tell*, in Italy in 1952; a business agent in the United States took him for more than a million dollars; his fortunes sagged mightily. More and more he felt he was done for as an actor. Wearily he moved through a few more privately written and produced films; they didn't do well in the United States. In Europe his reputation was as great as it was in the 1930s. The mid-1950s had been a time of illness, and his third marriage had deteriorated. Then came a much noted comeback period: his fine acting in *The Sun Also Rises* and in *Too Much, Too Soon*. It was now late in his career, and he went to Mexico to begin his autobiography. Writing about one's own life is difficult and his effort wasn't moving well. It was then he and I were brought together.

I think the title of his book, *My Wicked, Wicked Ways*, helped somehow to give a slightly incorrect impression of his character. The title was the artist in him, leaping for caricature and satire to produce effect. Apart from being nervous or irritable, or perhaps upset from his intoxicant intake, he did not treat individuals or the world in any "wicked" way.

It is quite possible that Errol was largely "wicked" primarily to himself. This has been remarked upon by many who knew him. His father wrote to me, "Errol was unjust to himself." One or two directors he was associated with said about the same thing. Director Lewis Milestone remarked, "His faults harmed no one but himself."

Ten weeks had gone by. The research stage of the book was largely completed. We were still around the hotel and Port Antonio, drifting, swimming, boating. The strange man's story drifted through me.

Once more, a final time, we went seeking the big snook.

He always talked of the snook as if it were the Loch Ness monster and quite a mystery.

I had developed a mild fear of it and wondered what would happen if the raft we were on tipped over and the big snook sharked off a thigh of mine.

"I've been searching for the big snook ever since I came to Jamaica," he explained. "He's here. He knows I'm looking for him."

Mostly he had caught foot-long fishes in a net. He brought them back to the hotel to be cooked up.

He would look momentarily disappointed on the way back when no big snook was there on the raft or being towed behind.

"What's it look like?" I asked once more.

He gave me a bleary look.

"How big is it?"

The same bleary look.

•   •   •

Brainstorm! What kind of a fish was the snook? This time I beat it into the hotel for a dictionary, but there was none. In town there was a library, I was told. I phoned. "Do you have a dictionary?" They had.

I called a cab.

Once there and with Webster in my hands I riffled the pages, found snool, snod, snood . . . there . . . there!

SNOOK, SNOWK (English dialect, *snook* to search out, to follow by the scent, from Middle English *snoken,* to sniff, smell): Scottish & Dialect, To sniff, to pry about.

Why, the sonofagun! A damned prank like everything else!

The snook was his big search, quest, wander junket. He didn't know what he was looking for anymore than I or anyone else.

In the remaining days, as he and I drifted about the hotel and its environs, made another rafting trip down the Rio Grande River, I had an even better opportunity to view him close up. He and I were together constantly, no Small Companion about. He talked and talked . . . so did I.

In the years since, flashes, memories, reminiscences have surfaced in me irrepressibly, how he behaved from minute to minute, things he said. . . .

. . . His favorite song was something that had the words "belly to belly" in it. I don't know what the song was, never heard the rest of it, don't know who wrote it and have made no effort to trace it. But it would burst from him in good humor from time to time: then he was all joy and self and his own reality. His most persistent dream of the most persistent self-satisfaction: belly to belly.

. . . It will come as a surprise to those who may have some image of Errol as a man with a wardrobe to hear that mostly, in the time I knew him, he wore only one suit, one or two different shirts and the same necktie all the time. The necktie with a jockey on a horse underneath the knot was frayed; the horse looked like a loser. I bought Errol a few new neckties; he said thanks, but never wore them. It didn't matter to him very much if his shirt and collar looked frayed and if the suit might or might not be pressed. Whatever he wore or didn't wear he always came through looking like Errol Flynn: his look being carried chiefly by the set and breadth of his shoulders, his erect walking style, the sword cane he carried. He could have been wearing rags, but he'd look the same way.

. . . I rarely saw him take a drink of water. "Water," he said, "is for swimming in."

. . . He was the only guy I ever saw take a drink of vodka, then a bite out of a chocolate bar, then another sip of the vodka, then another bite of the bar: and so on through a glass of the one and a bar of the other.

. . . He had a cat named Casanova. He gave his cat a vasectomy. "There are enough kittens in the world," he said, and added, "he can still have fun."

. . . He was an unabashed admirer of talent, especially versatility in a performer or any creator. If there was any one he respected above others, it was Charles Chaplin. His way of acknowledging that was to refer to Orson Welles, whom he also admired creatively, as "having Charlie Chaplin blood." He made this entry in his diary. "Rome 10th Feb. 1953: Today I saw Orson Welles: fat & bloated as Nero with no fiddle at his hedonistic best, but seemingly enchanted with himself and life. Possibly a front, this, but forthright enough. Intelligent, aggressive and no servant of bromides in life. He seems to me that fairly ambitious paradox, not at all uncommon: a man of large, perhaps great ability, able to dominate others, who is at the same time quite a bit of a fool. 'La betise n'est pas mon forte,' he seems to proclaim. The hell it isn't. Luckily no self-sanctity in Orson. But until he grows up mentally he is a fool. 'La betise' is precisely his 'strong point.' "

. . . Errol saw something in himself of John Barrymore, and at the last, when he was chosen to play Barrymore in *Too Much, Too Soon,* this was for him the realization of a histrionic dream. There, in a movie anyway, he had achieved eminence and equality with his theatrical inspiration. "I felt like John when I was playing his closing days. I felt I was living and dying at the same time. I felt I was him: the way he felt."

. . . He often used an expression about my writing I had never heard before, but it sounded like a Hollywoodism. "It's under your arms." I still don't know exactly what that meant. But I know that whenever I write or think hard at a typewriter, I sweat under the arms and have to change shirts in midwriting.

. . . Whenever he answered the telephone, his opening words were, "Be brief."

. . . Errol often said the most interesting people were not those who were realized or rich or famous but "the strugglers who are on their way up, who are alert, full of thought and of striving—they are the ones that add the verve in conversation and life."

. . . He believed the world was composed of the rulers and the ruled. When he demanded of a waiter, "Where is the chutney?" the tone of his voice contained a sword that was about to sunder the head and neck of the servant.

. . . He went around with $40,000 in cash in his pocket for several days in Jamaica. He wanted to buy up more land. He told me it was the only way he could hang onto his earnings. Otherwise it was taken from him or he threw it away. I don't think it was ever said of Errol that he was generous, that he gave—at least not money, not things. But he was taken for millions, by wives, business agents, business associates. It was hard for him to hang onto anything.

. . . One day he was walking by the swimming pool in front of the Titchfield—it was midday and the sun shone. He dived, fully dressed, into the pool, swam underwater, came up on the other side, crawled up on the cement siding dripping like a dog and went into the hotel, back up to his room and changed his clothes.

. . . He believed in "connections." He was often happy to use his offices as one who knew people, could phone them, intercede, get things done for others. He did that in an instant, ran to the phone, local call or long distance, to put in a good word for someone.

. . . He made me think sometimes: What's good? What's evil? What's right? What's wrong? What's legal? What's illegal? What's rich? What's poor? What's beauty? What's ugliness? Seeing him function from minute to minute made me speculate about the whole scheme, the whole value system or its valuelessness, caused me to wonder what made anything go, why it went as it did, how it had come along this far and where it was going next; convinced me how unplanned life is from birth to death: how we live each second, not knowing what the next will or should bring.

Something about him brought on this awareness because
he was alive in a moment of being, from one minute's being
to the next.

. . . What he hated most was boredom: the ogre that had
to be fought off from moment to moment. How to do it?
He woke each day knowing this was the challenge and
knowing that in some way special to himself, peculiar to his
own method of operation, the challenge would be met.
There was a simple principle involved: whatever you do, do
it differently. If it was done so differently that it amounted
to the abnormal or even the aberrant, the God of Boredom
had been punched in the jaw and you had won a bout with
another day. He believed that great films were created in
the same way: by a director who departed from the script
and added a peculiar or idiosyncratic touch of his own, the
right measure of unpremeditated creative aberration, the
mad touch.

. . . He said to me, "I don't believe there is anything in
the sea that will poison you." He meant that all in the sea
that moved could be eaten: the plankton by the fish, the fish
by man: the squid, the starfish, the oyster, even the Por-
tuguese man-of-war if properly prepared. He didn't believe
you could get a stomach-ache, a skin disease or anything
fatal from anything that crawled at the bottom of the sea,
or swam at the top or hung around a rock. He had that
certainty about the seas and the oceans of the world.

. . . His Small Companion, influenced by the master,
handed me a chocolate. I said thanks and popped it into my
mouth. When it was half-chewed, she asked, "You know
what that is?" I stopped chewing. "It's a chocolate-covered
grasshopper." I hawked and spit up the thing. Errol casti-
gated her sharply. "You have to know how to do those

things," he advised her. "Pranking is an art. Never offend the taste buds."

. . . There are many women in the world today who cherish the recollection of a moment or an hour with Errol. He lighted on women here and there with the accidental quality of a bee chancing unscheduled on flowers in a field.

. . . He had no faith. But he had a religion. It was a poet's religion, a kind of pantheism. "Let's get out in the sun," he would frequently say: sun, water, nighttime, moon, flowers, the sound of the bird of paradise, the sight of a stalk of bananas hanging from a tree, the sensation of heavy brush under his feet; feeling a cyclone coming in, breathing the wind of the cyclone, his eye following the gray swarm in the sky; dipping suddenly into the river and going underwater for ten or twenty strokes; looking up at clouds. He was like this all the time, with or without vodka in him. If there were any laws in the world he respected, they were only those of the universe, that made the whole thing go, which neither he nor anyone else understood: the beingness of all out-doors, to be able to wave at a hillside and note its rhythm. Neither Shelley nor Keats had more of a sense of natural beauty than Errol Flynn. Perhaps it was fitting for his own kind of "perfection" before the time when his dissipations set in and his body changed contours and began to look worn. It was not faith in golden rules or commandments necessarily, not even ethics and laws as we know them—but in an awareness of himself as elemental in a world of physical elements.

The day before we were to fly back to New York we made a last visit to Castle Comfort to see how the new house was coming along.

By now the base of the house was laid, the outlines of it visible in a rectangle of cement.

"You will occupy the guest room right over there," he said, motioning. "We will have a table in a small screened enclosure in back where we can do our collaborations."

He pointed to a spot only a few feet away, close to and in the rear of what would become the new big house. A tree would be planted there, an oak, and he said, "I want to be buried right there."

His raised arm and pointed finger held for many seconds as he stared at the spot.

I couldn't understand how a man who was building a big new expensive house was thinking so much of death.

NEW YORK AND CUBA

On the crowded plane back to the States I sat about five rows behind Errol on the opposite side. The stewardesses knew that the great Flynn was aboard, and I must be something or other because I was with him.

When we were well over the Caribbean one of the young ladies, a German and the prettiest, fell into talk with me. Our conversation became animated. Errol, up ahead, not being attended by anyone, began to fidget. He could hear the talk going on a few feet behind him.

Suddenly he swiveled in his seat, craned his neck and sneered, "He does have a certain charm and style, doesn't he?"

Boy, he said that loud.

Half a dozen necks twisted in our direction. The stewardess went momentarily quiet. I felt like finding a swift parachute.

Where had I heard that expression before, "a certain charm and style?" I had certainly heard him use it once before.

I recalled that Errol had, in the late 1950s, brought to
Jamaica one of the famous Deadend Kids. The particular
fellow had been a rowdy on some street corner in some big
city before he was co-opted for Hollywood and screen
fame; and he remained raucous on the screen and in his
private life. To Errol it was fun to have a roughneck around
him. And no competition whatever in any department.

So he took the Deadend Kid to Jamaica and had him
around Boston Estate for a while, where Errol's mother
watched him cavort. Marelle Flynn was outraged by the
shenanigans and language of this chap. She marveled at his
zip, his tricks and his capacity for pimento wine, which
equaled Errol's.

One day the perplexed Marelle Flynn said to her son,
with due sarcasm, "He does have a certain charm and style,
doesn't he?"

That had put Errol in his place. Now he put me in mine.

Though unsettled by the cozy way the German stewardess and I conversed, he wasted no time in giving her his
Warwick Hotel address. They agreed to meet the night
following the plane's arrival.

New York City had a catalytic effect upon him always. He
said it represented a place of violence for him: he associated only violent living with that city. All became cen-
trifuged: females, alcohol, drugs, incidents. Everything
must be countered, entered into, opposed.

He hated the place, but once in a while business drew
him there. His lawyer was in New York; there were matters
of his estate, business enterprises stemmed from the city.

In the succeeding weeks he alternated between New York
and Cuba.

First he must go to Havana to see his rich friends.

He was gone about three or four days. When he returned he looked drugged. He didn't give me details, but there had been sailboating and females, and he hardly knew what happened.

But something of the Jamaica "rest period" had gone from him and he was "living" again. I kept thinking about his remark, "If I have any genius it is for living," and the equally occasional remark he would make that his job was to defy the norms, not to stay within them; to experiment with the abnormal. This he called living, genius.

I was busy on the book, but Errol wanted me around when he was in the city. I must go downtown daily, pal around with him for a while, take in the Stork Club or go swimming with him at the Lexington Hotel pool. A friend of mine had given me a pass to that pool, to which I could have access daily. When I mentioned it to Errol and asked if he wanted a swim, he leaped at the opportunity. There he met another young lady, an attendant, a swimmer. Enough happened so that one of the columnists noted it.

One evening a couple of weeks after we were in New York and Errol had already been to Cuba and back, I received a phone call from the German stewardess he had dated on the plane. She said she was staying at the hotel with him. "I didn't know it was going to be like this," she gushed.

It was Errol's way of letting me know that he could still fly his own banner on any old plane.

Another time, when the German girl was back in New York from one of her trips, she walked into the Stork Club. He had told her this was where he could be located when she again arrived. He and I chanced to be there when I

Didn't Know It Was Going to Be Like This walked in.

I nudged Errol. "Look who's here."

He rose swiftly from our table, leaped three or four feet across the red carpeting and caught her up in an embrace that would have been appreciated by Bette Davis in *Essex.*

It was six in the evening and the bar was two or three deep with drinkers. Everyone watched the performance. Errol and the stewardess held that stance for many seconds, clasping, embracing, kissing. Errol always said he could never perform before a camera like that, but here at the club it was apparently different.

As they swirled out of the club she looked back at me and I screamed at them: "I DIDN'T KNOW IT WAS GOING TO BE LIKE THAT."

The phone in his Warwick Hotel two-room suite rang. Errol picked up the receiver.

I caught the gist from his expressions: Oh, we did meet in Spain? . . . Let me see, Marguerite? . . . yes, yes . . . m-m, nice of you to call. . . . Let me think. . . .

He didn't know who the devil the girl was but she had been on the *Zaca,* had dined with him, reminded him of a couple of things. When, after several minutes of trying to place her he still couldn't recall, he sensitively asked the payoff question, "Did we?"

She must have said yes, because he suddenly exclaimed, "Oh, we did. Wait a minute. Don't tell me, let me think another minute. Where was it?"

She must have told him.

He promised he would be around for a couple more days, and yes . . . they could meet at the hotel bar for a drink.

Putting the receiver back in place he said, "Ordinarily I'd

duck out of a reunion like that. What's happened has happened. But she's kind of nailed me. I'm hoping she's not got some little toddler along with her who'll scream, 'Da-da.' "

The maid entered to clean up his suite.

She was about forty, with that worn look that hotel maids often have. I don't recall that she was either pretty or not pretty. She was busying herself about the room, dusting, trying to ignore the presence of three men.

Then she moved into the bedroom to clean that room.

Errol followed her into the bedroom.

Errol's lawyer and I sat quietly, refracting the scene. I can't recall what conversation passed between the lawyer and myself, but we were acquainted, and there was always Errol to talk about or some allied matter.

The lawyer was there that morning to discuss a settlement of legal trouble Errol was having with Huntington Hartford, stemming from a play that Hartford had financed and Errol had walked out on.

There was an undue silence from the other room. Then we heard a curious sound as of mild remonstrance, a click of air, a fluff of something doing.

I had an idea what might be being attempted there. So did the lawyer.

I shrugged my shoulders: let's wait and see. The lawyer shrugged his: let's wait and see.

Those funny sounds continued.

Of a sudden the woman came tearing out of the bedroom, looking flustered, somewhat set upon. She gave us angry glances, then opened the door and sped on out to the hallway.

The lawyer and I needed no speech. Our look transferred the same thought back and forth between us: Errol was trying his luck, passing up nothing that wore a dress.

He came out a minute later, a mildly flushed look upon his features. He shrugged his shoulders.

Errol and I were descending in the elevator at the Warwick. In the lift with us was a couple: a woman in her forties and her husband of the same age. Errol began a flirtation with the woman: first hot glances, he assaying her from hair to foot; smiling, bowing, indulging in conventionalities of no consequence.

The woman was obviously stirred and disturbed at the attentions from this so charming and looming a figure. Her husband stood by, in a corner of the elevator, stoic but fully alert to the telegraphy between this big handsome character and his wife who, I thought, must only rarely be the recipient of such special attentions in street, elevator or anywhere else.

I can't even recollect her face. She was a woman. What else can I report?

In the lobby Errol marched ahead of all of us. The woman grabbed me by the arm. "Who *is* that man!"

"Errol Flynn."

She hurried, like a trim yacht with a wind behind her, and met him at the door. They fell into swift heated converse.

The husband, at his own pace, drew close but did not disrupt the volcanic talk—volcanic on her part.

Out of the corner of his eye Errol saw the frustrated husband, and he knew a killer air when it was close by. This man could be troublesome. That's the way the scene looked to me, too.

I stayed about fifteen feet behind the other three and

couldn't hear what Errol and this woman said to each other.

Once more Errol allowed his glance to settle upon the face and figure of the quiet husband.

I'll bet nothing comes of this, I said to myself.

Nothing ever did.

Later, Errol, talking about that moment, said to me, "I've considered much about the best way of dying, but I don't like bullets."

That wasn't exactly true. In approaching days, as Castro began his military takeover of Cuba, Errol would join up in that campaign precisely—I think—to catch a bullet.

There was the night of the gathering of his flunkies. They were New Yorkers who, when he got there, came to see and to be with him. Whether he called them, or how they learned he was in town, I wouldn't know. But he had a way of being swiftly surrounded by ten or fifteen of the most ordinary folk in the world, people who weren't like him at all: there would be pretty girls all blonde and nineteen or twenty, a few racetrack types, one or two figures of great wealth, someone from the media. They each deemed it a great thing to be part of the company of Flynn. The flattery brushed off on each in a way that said: You too are significant. They weren't. Maybe they had worked, maybe they were bums, maybe they were hookers. They were all idling types. For days they would circle like moths around Errol Flynn's light.

They paid no attention to me. I wanted none, expected none. I was simply curious about the scene. Why did Errol need their attention, adulation, the look of affection they had for him?

On this night he was wildly drunk. I had never seen him

that way before. He reeled, he stumbled, he fell, he tossed himself on a divan, half rolled off, but stood up and moved toward the table of drinks, chattered and chatted. His eyes seemed lighted, like small electric bulbs. All about were his "friends."

This was his response to being in New York: It was go go go.

Late in December 1958 I learned that Errol was with Fidel Castro as the latter began the last phase of his march to oust Fulgencio Batista, the dictator of the island. News reports arrived daily of guerilla-style fighting, of the retreat of Batista's troops. Then, on January 1, 1959, Batista fled Cuba and Fidel became premier.

Errol had gone as a correspondent but also as one who disliked dictatorship and didn't care for Batista. He had had good times gambling and drinking in Havana and he liked the Cubans.

Now he was in Cuba: the violence, the horror, the politics, the upheaval interested him. He had an affinity for such conditions.

His Cuban friends had arranged for Errol to meet Castro; he was attending Castro's meetings and moving about with the revolutionary troops—and a photographer.

Dhondi was in Cuba with him but was at the Commodore in Havana awaiting the return of her revolutionary.

One day I received a phone call from her from a midtown New York apartment. "We're back. Come down to this address." She gave me the address of an apartment belonging to a friend of Errol's.

In half an hour I was there, waiting in the living room for the revolutionist—or whatever he now was—to come out of the bath.

When he emerged I hardly recognized him. He had lost weight; he was as slim as he had been at twenty-five. His face was drawn, haggard and starved into leanness. But there was a brilliance about him I hadn't ever seen; it was the look of a man who had done something.

I stretched out my hand. "Lord Byron," I said.

He blossomed into a wide smile. I had hit a profound inner chord. Here was a touch of the early poet, the dreamer who wanted to be in the British Parliament perhaps, or to be famed in some other public way in his motherland. And he had gone and done what Byron had once done.

Errol Flynn was back from "Greece."

He believed that he was living one of those roles he had played in the movies, and he felt good about having done something real and not being a "ham"—that terrible word of the theatrical world.

In the next few days he recounted his adventures in Cuba and I put them into a series of articles that were published in this country and throughout Europe.

Someone in England sent him a four-column cartoon from an English newspaper satirizing the presence of Hollywood stars during the Cuban revolution. The cartoon was published at a time when there was worldwide comment on Errol being in Cuba with Castro. George Raft's name was mentioned in the media too as he had spent much of his time and money gambling on that island. But Errol's presence "on the march" with Fidel carried more interest.

The cartoon showed a busty American actress, a combination of Jayne Mansfield and Marilyn Monroe, and in the cartoon the name of the actress was a combination of these two. The bosomy actress, scantily clad, was perched on the head of an elephant which, in turn, was carried on a platform forty or fifty feet long by a retinue of serfs. The bearers were carrying the Hollywood heroine onto the battlefield, and underneath the cartoon was the caption: We Hollywood Ladies Have Got to Help Our Boys in Cuba.

Very laughable at the time. And perhaps still laughable. Rather a real picture of what Errol might be doing there in the front lines, giving a Hollywood touch to the serious business of bringing about social change on the island.

Errol, with a sly smile in his eyes, handed me the cartoon. "What do you think of this?" he asked.

I went into a peal of laughter.

"It's pretty good, isn't it?" he said.

There was a surge of new spirit in him. The war correspondent role. He must go back to Cuba, be present as Castro took over, report the scene, send back correspondence. "I will send it to you," he said. "You will put it in shape. Maybe I can get to do a column for a chain of newspapers."

He was reverting to his origins, to the time in the late 1920s when he was a reporter for an Aussie paper, The Sydney *Bulletin,* from New Guinea; reliving his forsaken literary dream.

And he did return to Cuba. There he undertook to make a last film, *Cuban Rebel Girls.*

Weekly he wrote me his reactions, thinking they might make material for feature articles or for a column he hoped he and I would be doing together. He had a few words about Friday, February 13, 1959, when he witnessed some executions:

I have witnessed many gruesome sights in my life, but none more so than a human facing a firing squad. I don't care how much he deserves it, it made me vomit—and I couldn't have given a damn when I saw the expressions of faint amusement on the faces watching the hero of a thousand screen battles, Flynn, go white and heave his brave guts up. Brave? Guts? I puked—gagged close to the feet of a guard, spilling on the end of his hardworn boot, and there was a faint amusement in the faint flicker of the smile he had. It was in Oriente Province, Cuba—it happened; a thing I'll never watch again. (Unless, perchance, my masters, I happen to be on the wrong end of the guns.)

He and Dhondi were staying at the Commodore Hotel in Havana, and from there, on March 30, 1959, he described his interview with an American executioner, Luke Beryll, employed by the Cubans to shoot condemned Batistans:

You will note this is in very rough shape, and I haven't time to do more about it. Have a go at it, if you think it's worthwhile. The same deal as always, of course, between us. Let me know if you need more details. If so, what kind.

Luke Beryll has eyes that remind me of a tiger, except that they are blue. His four front teeth are missing from the top, and it is said that when he gives the coup de grace, instead of one bullet, he will empty a magazine into the back of the condemned man's head, dead or alive. That's hear-say. It was hard to get Beryll to open up about his job. Harder still to get to talk to him, so our meeting had to be sort of "hush-hush," cloak and dagger stuff. The present Cuban regime is not fond of having these executions written about.

Beryll did not remind me of the Lord-high executioner in the Mikado, and somebody was pretty smart in the government by putting an American in charge of blowing out Cuban brains, don't you think?

In haste.

Love to you all,
Errol Flynn

P.S.—I am pretty sure the six-rifle squad does not enjoy its job. The wall against which the condemned are lined up is splattered with bullet holes that have not passed through human flesh. Also, here in Cuba you are not shot in the traditional European way: that is, that one rifle of the squad has a blank in it so that no one man knows who had the blank. Here all the guns are loaded and perhaps that accounts for the bullet holes in the wall behind the guy who has got to get it.

Beryll visited Flynn in his suite, he wrote later, and told him that no women and no cameras were allowed at the executions. Beryll said the rebel girls did no actual fighting, but cooked, sewed and nursed. If they were caught with men, it meant a marriage right on the spot. Errol asked Beryll if he could photograph him doing his job. "No," the man said. "The worst job and most dirty is mine. It is a job I do not personally like, but somebody has to do it." They talked about torture and Beryll said he was against it. Errol told him, "You must know why I am here, buddy. I am trying to get an article." Beryll said he had seen Errol's articles in the Havana *Post.* Errol asked Beryll why he had risked his life coming to Cuba, adding, "I risked my own, by the way, when it came to coming down here." Beryll said he had been coming to Cuba a long time and had learned to like the country.

All that talk had been preliminary to Errol asking what to him was now a very important question: shouldn't a condemned man have the choice of the way he wanted to die —firing squad, hanging, guillotine, cyanide, gas chamber or something else? Beryll said the way to go was the firing squad.

Errol's dialogue with Beryll ended this way:

FLYNN: "Would you rather have the firing squad?"

BERYLL: "Yes."

FLYNN: "What do you think that man feels when he sees those black holes pointed at him? What does the man think and say?"

BERYLL: "He always says to shoot him in the heart."

FLYNN: "Don't you think it would be better to have a doctor come in and say, "You Bastard, etc., you are a criminal—*voilà!*" I would prefer that. You look away, a needle goes in and you are finished. I am very interested in your opinion. Don't you think it would be better to give that guy a choice?"

BERYLL: "Did he give the people he killed a chance or a choice?"

FLYNN: "Guess not."

BERYLL: "Then why should he have an alternative?"

FLYNN: "Then let me ask you this: Jesus Christ said if you are hit by a man you should turn the other cheek."

BERYLL: "Would you?"

FLYNN: "No. Hell no—I'll go down fighting when my hour strikes."

Errol included a list of choices of the manner of death for condemned persons. He asked:

Why shouldn't condemned criminals be allowed to look at a list something like this:

1. Cyanide pills (Goering Nazi War Criminal) inserted in rectum at will

2. Lethal dose of morphine (best way out)

3. Choice of drowning with a half-ton weight attached to feet

4. Being dropped out of a helicopter from about fifty feet on rocky place by the sea

5. Getting into cage with sex-starved gorilla

6. Injections, voluntary of course, of caviar (gray eggs, of course) by nose, mouth, ear or rectum.

Errol went on: "I admonish any civilized legislature in
this day and age to pause before denying anyone the
human right of the condemned to choose his or her manner
of dying. What's it matter? One man I saw, with seconds to
go, had a sore throat (and I have this on film) and seemed
bothered about the black silk handkerchief around his
neck. This sore throat was bothering him and he died,
bothered, as the six rifles barked. . . .

"So you see, all this poses a problem when it comes to
my execution, which could be any day now, and I have so
few suggestions to offer, except the needle. I don't know.
Painless, practical even. Perhaps pleasant."

Errol ended his ruminations and theorizings about
death, condemned men and official murders this way:

This is why, having seen men's bellies and chests riddled, not
in cold blood, but in hot blood, understandable after a revolution, I feel very strongly a man should be permitted to choose his
own Exit, his own way. He should be given something like a
menu, with suggestions on the à la carte Bill of Fare. And I am
not being facetious.

There he was, wholly real, but part-facetious in spite of
himself, and most of all wondering about his own demise,
which he must have felt was not far away.

Yet his concern for death made me wonder whether it
was possible that his expression of it might really be an
ardent desire to live on and quite the opposite from what
it seemed to be: a snooking out of the Great End.

Is it possible, I thought, that people who read obituary
notices, who worry (as he did) about how much space
would be given to his hour of passing (he estimated two or
three days of steady banner lines: he was right)—was such

a person in actuality so much in love with the act of living
that he feared dying, feared parting with life, and wanted
simply to go on and on, obviously an ancient and universal
urge?

Hadn't he mused in one of his early letters how sad it
might be not to be around two hundred years later to keep
enjoying the sensations of the day? Hadn't he wondered
often how many of his pictures might endure, might be
reshown, how often his face and form and sword might
again swash across the screen? He had.

Was it possible that a man could be so in love with living
that the biggest dread of his life might somehow become
the fear and the realization of his end and a desire, as Dylan
Thomas put it, not to go gentle into that good night.

Is it in the presence of such energies that the Great Fear
obtrudes harshly, terribly, and possesses some people?

I for one cannot figure whether he wanted to live or die,
or which he wanted more to do.

After he finished making *Cuban Rebel Girls,* in the spring
of 1959, he and Dhondi headed back to Jamaica to see what
the new house would look like and to rest up for a while.
For a month they lived in the new house. He and Dhondi
sent me a long, garrulously written personal note to let me
know the zany and wonderful time they were having in
Jamaica. They would soon be coming to New York and
would fill me in on more details. It was a love note to me
and did not have any bearing on the book, although I was
now near the end of my writing stint. But he did go into
detail about something that titillated him very much. He
poured out some pleasurable vitriol about mama, same old
feud. He wrote:

My mother has just turned seventy-five and claims to be a
pillar of the Church, a fount of wisdom. There is no subject
upon which she is not an authority, and my father had better
look out for himself if perchance a coarse word every now and
again escapes his loose jaw in a moment of convivial happiness.
He is likely to crack out with terrible oaths like "damn" or "the
hell with you," at which one of them my mother who has ears
like an owl at night just bends one frightening stare on the old
professor and he sinks into the obscurity from which he should
never have emerged. Mother, her spry seventy-five, still goes
swimming at Boston Bay beach in Jamaica where I live, and
punishes the rolling breakers there as she would me or my father or anybody else who got in her way. She has always been
a frustration to me because it appears she is always right and
can prove it conclusively.

Certainly this was a fifty-year war. Certainly it was at the
roots of Errol. Now he was delighted to discover a discrepancy between the day of his parents' marriage and the date
of his birth.

. . . Looked up my birth certificate, a photostat of which I
reproduce here, and at the age approaching fifty I find that I
narrowly missed illegitimacy. Read it for yourself. I am quite sure
that my mother will have a ready answer for the discrepancy
between my birth and her marriage. I have written Mother a sort
of congratulatory note, although we are hardly on speaking terms
let alone writing terms for the last forty years. I just put her one
mild question since she is rather old now, but still can swim better
than me: "Was I an incubator baby in 1909? I figured that they
didn't have such things." In other words I must have been desperately premature—by five months. As you will note, the birth
in the District of Tasmania, Hobart: a child, sex—male; was born
20th of June, 1909, at the Alexandria Hospital. It says Name and
Surname, Age and Birth Place of Father—Theodore Thompson
Flynn, 25 years; Mother's Name and Surname, When and Where

Married, Age, Birth Place—Marelle Thompson Flynn (she changed her name from Lily Mary, but that is O.K.) Young, January 23, 1909, Sydney, 21 years of age. Rank or Profession of Father—Lecturer in Biology. Next her format, signature, description, residence: T. Theodore Thompson Flynn, Father, Warwick Street (wherever the hell that is), 31st July, 1909.

It is strange looking at this document that says:

> I certify that the above is true from the Book of Births in the State of Tasmania given at the Registrar General's Office in Hobart on the 2nd day of April, 1936.

I note the jolly discrepancy. In other words, I have Mother nailed to the mast at last and she is going to have a tough time getting out of this one, but no doubt she will, being a woman of infinite plausibility resource.

When Married, it says here on my birth Certificate No. 10472, January the 23rd, 1909; Born, Errol Flynn, June 20, 1909. Oh, Mother! Really, how could you! Why don't you let me in on some of these secrets? I will never betray you to the Church of which you are a pillar; but why, my darling Mother, did you don the garb of the Virgin Mary. . . . Mother, darling, I have never pretended to be "holier than thou," but G . . . d . . . it, I must say you make me laugh when I saw my birth certificate just now. Of course, you will have some explanation, and of course, whatever it is it doesn't matter because I am nearly 50, but please stop building churches with belfries. . . .

Errol had a mortal hatred of his mother's religious protestations, her rectitude, her properness, her sense of outrage at the way he lived, her constant chastising him about his choice of young girls, her fear of another statutory rape case. She was always talking about the church; she had helped to build one in Jamaica, and she was in love with church bells.

Now he had her!

It had taken him fifty years.

●   ●   ●

In Jamaica Errol again felt that he was seriously ill, that he needed expert medical attention. That would be in New York.

Besides, his book was being set in type now and he would have to be around to read galleys.

He arrived in Manhattan, took an apartment downtown and at once entered Columbia Presbyterian Hospital at 168th Street and Broadway. That was near where I lived, so I got over there right away.

He was sitting up in bed in his hospital room but he looked shot. His face was bloated. He seemed dizzy and he behaved dizzily. That was understandable because he had been suffering with vertigo intermittently from a long time back.

But the old resonance in his voice wasn't there. In a low, strained utterance he said: "I-think-I-have-cancer-of-the-throat."

He stared at me and I stared back at him.

"Errol," I said after a pause, "if you die of cancer you'll disappoint millions of people."

His eyes, which rarely rounded, now did.

Then and there I knew he would never die of cancer of the throat because I could simply feel him making up his mind not to disappoint millions of people.

He began to pick up from that minute.

The next day things were even better.

In spite of X rays, tube examinations of his esophagus and other tests, in spite of being sedated by various medications, he was managing a bout in bed with his Small Companion when, alas, a nurse knocked on the door and entered in time to see the stricken patient in a paroxysm—not of death, but of life.

On the third day one of his racetrack pals, an Italian chap, Marty, whom he had known in Rome, came rushing into the room. Errol had given Marty some betting money to put on one horse or another at the Monmouth Race Track and Marty had been lucky with it.

He tore into the room like the winning horse itself and poured bills all over Errol's face and head, yelling, "Long shot! Long shot! Long shot!"

The bills—ones, fives and tens—fell all over Errol's face and stomach.

Errol sat up electrified. He echoed unbelievingly, "Long shot? Long shot? Long shot?"

He looked like a revivified King Midas. Though he had a couple of million dollars worth of coconut land in Jamaica, this rain of unexpected winnings made him ecstatic.

He rolled around in the bills like a little boy tumbling in a sandbox. Some greenbacks fell off the bed and he and Marty bumped heads reaching for them. The bed covers had been white; now they were speckled rectangular green. Bills caught under Errol's neck, vanished between his thighs. He scrambled them about as if they were golden eggs.

I had a hunch Marty had collected the winnings in the smallest possible denominations to make the bundle look more impressive.

The bills came to rest, several hundred bucks worth—I heard Marty say "Four hundred!" Anyway, it was enough to delight Errol.

In fact, he was cured.

"Sport," he said, turning to me, "I'm getting out of here tomorrow."

What ailed him specifically at this time I don't know. Perhaps his heart. But I felt that his sense of survival was enormous and I expected nothing imminently.

My Wicked, Wicked Ways was finished and in galleys. Errol and I spent about three weeks going over the book line by line at the Shoreham Hotel on West 55th Street where he had an apartment.

One day he had four girls draped around beds and chairs reading chapters of the book. I walked in and was astounded to see the layout of young females he had cornered to do a final job upon the autobiography we had worked so hard to create.

"Look, Errol," I remonstrated, "this is no way to go about editing the galleys. Maybe that's the way they do it in Hollywood, with a bevy of broads going over the scenarios, but I'm not used to that."

"Don't you think it's a good way to wind up the book?" he asked.

I felt outraged.

I looked at one girl. She was on the bed, four or five sheets of paper in her left hand, a pencil in her right. She wet the lead on the tip of her tongue and blithely went ahead making notations on the script.

I looked into an adjoining room. There was another lying on her stomach, her backside to me, sprawled for action, but the only action she was engaged in was penciling some other chapter of the book.

I returned to the main room where Dhondi was looking over some pages. A typist was at work in another corner, gravely editing *My Wicked, Wicked Ways.*

I said, "Goddamnit, Errol, you and I have never argued, but this is where I draw the line. You throw them all out!"

Errol laughed. "All right, girls, give the copy back." One by one the girls got off their beds and their butts and brought the pages and chapters to him.

"Feel better, sport?" he asked.

The phone rang. Errol picked up the receiver. From time to time he said yes, he might be interested, that was fine. He agreed to meet with a couple of men at a nearby hotel on the following day.

Errol explained it was a television show, thirty-nine weeks if it ran well, and first came making a pilot film and figuring out what the deal might be. It was Caribbean stuff; he would be a deep-sea diver and have romances with young ladies waiting for him to surface.

"It'll probably come to crap," he said, "but I have to go through these paces. Prospective deals like this come along frequently and you have to look into them if they talk big enough."

The next day Errol and his entourage of myself and his lawyer met with two businessmen.

I heard large figures being tossed around, a quarter million, percentages, reruns, much talk that probably made them all feel good.

"Are you in shape to do this?" asked one of the men, looking over Errol closely, his paunch, his mottled complexion. "Did that Cuba stint wear you out?"

"Gentlemen, I've made more than fifty films, I can make thirty more." Then, as an afterthought, "Not that I'm all that interested in your proposition."

"What's the matter with it?"

"Nothing. But I've been undersea quite a bit this year. I may need a stand-in or two to do some of that work."

"That could be arranged."

"One other thing."

"Yes?"

"In any inside tank where there is close-up filming, where there are close shots of me tangling with the swords of swordfish, the tanks must be filled with a special vitalizing substance."

"What's that?"

"Smirnoff."

Everybody broke into laughter.

There was no deal and afterward Errol said to me, "I knew it would be crap."

"It's Errol Flynn Day tomorrow at Monmouth. Would you go out there with me, Earl?"

"Wouldn't think of missing it."

The next morning I called at the Shoreham and he came out of his room dressed up, ready for the day at the race-track when he, a famous handicapper, would be honored by the regional horse-racing fans.

But he looked very sad. "I feel unlucky today," he opened.

"How so? It's a big day, you're getting honored."

"I feel unlucky. I think I'm going to lose a lot of money."

"You don't have to bet, do you?"

"I do. I've never gone to a racetrack where I didn't bet. Today I have the feeling I'll be betting heavily and I'll lose, and I'll be paying for that damned honor."

"Can't you decide for once not to place any bets?"

"I don't see how. Can I quit drinking? Can I stay off the

other?" He meant by that his drugs.

"You mean it's another of your addictions?"

"I'll bet today and I'll drop thousands, I'm sure."

A little later two beautiful girls showed up: so did a limousine that would take us all out to the New Jersey racetrack.

Errol, his two girls and I sat in the rear of the limousine, and the chauffeur was up front with one other person, one of Errol's male flunkies, this one an expert on horses.

As we went through the countryside, Errol viewed the green beauty of that late summer scene, and he waxed rhapsodic as I had seen him do often in Jamaica. Here was the poet in him, the nature poet, the Wordsworthian: a figure unknown and unrecorded by the screen magazine writers. For half an hour he studied the hills and ignored the girls, as I ignored the hills and studied the girls.

The Flynn party had a special box near the track, not far from the officials. There was a big banner that floated across the racetrack at the point where the races would start:

ERROL FLYNN DAY

The events opened with Errol down front standing beside one of the officials, who said a few words of praise about the presence of the great cinema star. He spoke through a megaphone, but nobody could hear what he said.

A little girl handed Errol a bouquet of flowers.

Every seat in the grandstand was occupied. There was a lot of applause. The fans stood. Errol nodded. It ought to have been a pleasant moment for him, but I knew he still suffered from that morning depression.

For the next couple of hours he kept leaving our box to

place bets. After the first hour he said, "I told you so. I've already dropped five thousand bucks."

"Can't you place smaller bets?"

"No. I have to have the big winning. I'm playing the long shots. They're all dogs. They're genuine long shots."

"One long shot now and you'd recoup, wouldn't you?"

"With the money I'm placing I'd walk off with thirty or forty thousand if a long shot came in."

But he kept losing.

He lost eight thousand dollars.

He paid no attention to the two beautiful girls who were on each side of him. His mind was on the horses, on his money, and he didn't seem to savor the great honor of the day.

I rose and said, "I'm restless. I'll meet you all at the limousine."

I reached the limousine and waited there for the reappearance of the day's hero.

Soon he came along. He looked so typically Errol Flynn as he approached with the two lovelies alongside.

Only he and I knew how unlucky a day it had been.

Errol pulled a letter out of his inside pocket, that pocket behind his question mark. He said, "Read it. It's from a girl who's trying to take my pants off."

"What?"

"A Spanish girl wants to take off my pants."

"What in hell . . ."

"Here, read this . . ."

Though I rarely saw him receive mail, a letter had somehow caught up with him at the Shoreham.

This Spanish girl wrote to him from Barcelona.

After pleasant opening amenities she described herself
as a very very pretty Spanish girl.

I'm very pretentious? Yes, very much!!! I shall explain the purpose of my letter!!

Today I have seen a film by you! Yes! The name I think is "The
Pirate's Island." By E. Flynn and Maureen O'Hara. It is a very,
very nice film! True!!!

My motive: In the last part of the film where you come to the
pirate's ship, after you see the Princess of Onningz and you're
fighting and smiting the pirates and with their captain and Miss
O'Hara is fighting too.

In this scene you wear a pair of blue velvet breeches.

I just think that the colour and tissue would suit me. Could you
send them to me? It is a foolish idea I know. . . . Do you ever come
to Spain?

I have to say good-bye. Will you write to me please?
Good night
Delfinia Morella

Sure, the gals always wanted to take the pants right off
him.

We were on our way to the Hotel Lexington swimming
pool, an every afternoon walk. Many recognized him,
looked hard and went on; others slowed. He enjoyed the
diverse reactions or was, sometimes, impervious. He handled his sword cane casually.

Toward us came a man screaming his head off, denounc-
ing the world, and in some way special to himself halting
every ten feet, saluting, then cursing. Errol slowed. He
stared hard. I had seen similar sights a thousand times and
ignored them: so do most New Yorkers.

"Let's duck in here," he said, grabbing me by the wrist

and turning into the entrance of the closest office building.

Inside he asked, "Has he gone by?"

"Not yet," I said.

"I can't stand that kind of sight."

He explained that when he was a kid in Hobart a friend of his took him to a local institution for the insane and showed him a certain room. Glancing through a small window, Errol viewed the human wrecks within: madmen thrown in with each other, faces twisted, excrement about them on the floor, eyes vacant or frenzied, half or all unaware. He had been horrified at that kind of end.

Errol's own experiences in hallucination or far-outness from drugs and alcohol had brought him close enough to these conditions so that lunacy was, along with castration, a major dread.

I didn't then understand how deep-seated the phobia was. I recalled that he had told me of that childhood experience in the course of our research.

But now one other recollection came to mind. This had happened nine or ten months earlier, after the first few hours we were together, during that turbulent plane ride to Jamaica.

We were only five hundred miles from Jamaica and because we had all been silent Errol, seeking conversation, asked if I could recommend one of my books for him to read. I didn't know just what might fit his taste so I spoke of the last work I had published a year or so earlier, *Mr. Seward for the Defense.* Knowing that he was from another part of the world, I explained that Seward had been Lincoln's Secretary of State, a post he held for eight years, and that he was a statesman in the tradition of the Founding Fathers. I told him that Seward, a great attorney, had initiated the first acknowledged legal defense of an accused murderer on grounds of insanity. William Freeman, a black ex-slave, had knifed in a mindless way a family of four, including two infants, in a small town in Central New York 125 years earlier. Seward for the first time in court history introduced experts—before the word "psychiatry" was invented—to project the idea of mental illness as a reason for murderous behavior, and the case became an historical precedent.

I went that far, and was looking at Errol in a sidelong way as he sat beside me.

I noticed that his right hand began to wave back and forth in a short parameter of a few inches, in a negative way. A sound came from some innermost portion of him. "No, no. I can't hear of . . . I can't read of insanity. It's just something I . . . not that one."

The waving of his hands in that definitive manner suggested to me that I had tread on some dangerous and personal ground. I retreated from the discussion quickly, and we fell into silence.

Now there was this street scene where he was unlike himself, it seemed to me, for he never feared to face anything. But he couldn't look even momentarily at this deranged man who behaved so peculiarly, so brain-lost.

"It's okay now, Errol," I said, looking about and no longer seeing the man, only the crowded New York street. "We can go now."

One day when we were looking over the galleys of the book he penciled in three words at the end of a certain sentence: *go go go.*

I had never heard the triple expression. I wasn't that hip.

"Errol," I said, *"three* go's?"

"Yes, three go's. Go go go."

"Aren't two enough?"

"No." He looked at me as if there was something I didn't know, as if I were ignorant. Which I was. This was 1959 and I had never heard the expression "go go go," but it was known in the Hollywood set; the go-go set had become the go-go-go set.

I don't remember how that was finally set up in *Wicked Ways,* whether with two go's or three, but Errol was himself go go go.

He had to go and to keep going. It dawned on me that he never stayed still very long, not for more than a few minutes or a few hours. Then he had to go to his boat, or go below water, or go to the bar, or go see a friend, or go to Cuba, or go to New York, or go to Hollywood, or go to England, or go to his estate, or go to the pool, or go ride a horse, or go to a party, or go in a plane, or go in a sailboat, or go in a motorboat, or go in a limousine, or go to a whorehouse, or go somewhere and go do something.

The going was part of his expenditure, his excess, his need to lose awareness of himself; not to find self-awareness, but to go from it and to pursue the hedonism that used up that early high-minded drive.

Having written about a few theatrical and cinema notables and other people in the world of doers, I have often been chagrined to hear them described as shy, or even to speak of themselves that way. I have found no shyness in any well-known or world-known figure. Shyness would be an anomaly. Yet you can hardly read an article about any of these screen strivers or producers without coming across that trademark of the hard-pressed public relations man: "Bonzo is essentially a shy man."

Shyness my eye.

I never saw anything about Errol that was shy. Shy people don't do the things Errol did on and off the screen. Yet one day his Small Companion got off that line to me, "He's really a shy person."

I once asked Dorothy Dandridge, whose autobiography I wrote with her, if she was shy. She truthfully answered no. But shortly afterward I read a magazine piece that described her as essentially shy. Imagine Duke Wayne being shy with another cowboy as he utters, "Saddle up!" Or Burt Lancaster shy while playing opposite equally shy Barbara Stanwyck.

No, these people are never shy.

When Errol was reading galleys of his book he said, "I see a lot of 'I's' on every page. Can't we get away from that?" He seemed downright resentful of the word "I."

"Errol," I explained, "it's an autobiography. It is first person. The only word and letter known for that is 'I.' You are telling your story. It has to be there sometimes. The only exception I know to that is Marian Anderson's autobiography. She used the word 'we' throughout. But she never fooled anybody. 'We' was she."

We cut a few "I's" from a few pages and he felt better, but he wanted to play the role of non-ego for a minute, the shy glamourist.

August 1959: a year had passed since we met. Corrected galleys were at the printer's.

Errol phoned to say he was sending a letter that contained an item about Jack Warner, an episode about his friend Dr. Gerrit Koets and a note about his Small Companion. He talked for a minute or two about a fourth item. "I'm enclosing a will, Earl. I want it run at the end of the book. I think that would be nice."

"A will? At the end of the book?"

There was already a pretty good ending, I thought, and a will would be anticlimactic. Also I knew of only one autobiography that ended with a will. Thurlow Weed, the kingpin political boss of the founding Republican Party, who amassed a fortune during the Civil War, left a will in which he specified that upon his death any male child anywhere to be named Thurlow was to receive a gift of a hundred dollars from his estate. That was a legally drawn will and it was carried out, too.

But a will at the end of *My Wicked, Wicked Ways?*

"Send it along anyway, Errol."

The will arrived, with a letter.

The Shoreham
33 West 55th St.
New York 19

Aug. 1, 1959

Dear Earl:
The enclosed episodes about Jack Warner, Koets and My Small Companion should be inserted and edited. Also find enclosed a piece which I think may be a good ending for the book.
Let's talk about it.

Yours,
Errol

I phoned the editor and said I was not in favor of adding a will to the end of the book. He was against it too and said the script was at the printer's. "Let's forget about it." I put the will aside, but told Errol that neither the editor nor I thought it a good idea.

The will was destined to become known for years, right to the present, as "the missing will."

A few months later when it was announced over the radio that Errol was dead in Vancouver, I took the will to my attorney, who took one look at it, said it was not legally drawn, it was unsigned, the accompanying letter with his signature was insufficient, and I didn't have to enter it for probate.

Errol had couched the will in his usual zany language, and I believe it was either a prank or a misdirected literary thought. Others in the Flynn family now also believe that it was one of his pranks. But for years all through the Flynn clan it has been supposed that a legally drawn will was left with someone, that it was missing and that it might one day surface.

Here is the will surfacing. Remember, it is unsigned, unwitnessed and I could do nothing with it but preserve it as another bit of memorabilia.

The will was preceded by a note:

PUBLISHED EXCERPTS OF WILL AT THE END OF "MY WICKED, WICKED WAYS"

My friend and lawyer, a realist, just yesterday shocked me with the startling news that I might one day die. I should draw up a will, he said. "Draw Up"? You draw up a bucket from a well, don't you? Or draw up something from the ocean bottom, or draw a mug of beer. Anyway, after his friendly counsel, one day early at dawn, I got on a horse named, incidentally, Evening Star, and took a fast gallop down to Boston Bay Beach, Jamaica, where the blue-white topped waves come in on the white sand and there's nobody around except some fishing canoes and dogs scratching themselves on the sand and there, after I had kicked my horse in the blue breakers, I sat down under a tree and tried to write a will on some toilet paper I had brought along for dual purposes.

[My lawyer] has carefully preserved this document which he claims should belong in the Archives of some legal Smithsonian Institute, if there is such a thing.

Dear Jew:
RE: my kids:

1. Sean?—OK, taken care of.
2. Deidre?—OK, taken care of.
3. Rory?—OK, taken care of.
4. Arnella—Not yet, properly.

(Darling brats of mine)
Maybe others yet to appear on stage????
RE: Mothers of kids.
They're God damn well taken care of, aren't they? They saw to that themselves, didn't they.
RE: Mother and Father.
In good shape, no worries there, but the old bitch still annoys the hell out of me.

FOR MY "SMALL COMPANION"
(If the little bitch is still around when I kick off) A half a million bucks. She has been nice and kind to me, we have to take good care of her, get it, I'm not being apologetic.

As for what's left the hell with it, anyone can have it who needs it, you fix it up. But don't give it to anyone but bums down on their luck and who the hell else needs it anyway where I'm going? The pretty secretary typing this just observed she could use some, so why don't we give her some? Especially as I just noticed her outspoken attractive tits lean over the typewriter at an engaging angle, but that's beside the point, or points. Legal Eagle, get going. Be sure that my two little girls are protected from eager

predators hotly after their dough I leave them. Sean's OK, knows
how to handle himself.

Best pal,
Errol

P.S. Anyone who comes to my funeral is automatically cut out of
my will . . . and I mean it. I absolutely hate the idea of well loved
people being subjected to the maudlin, sloppy, bullshit Lov ya,
Flynn of some priest or minister spouting off hurriedly over my
grave and wanting to get home to lunch.

My lawyer now asserts that my will has put him at a disadvan-
tage, legally speaking. Rereading it, legally speaking, who gives
a damn? He maintains I know little about how to write a will and
should not be allowed out with more than fifty bucks in my pants
pocket, if that.

To anyone who hoped to benefit from "the missing will"
I can only say sorry. It was merely one of Errol's last howls.

To the end he was vitally interested in his public image
and in keeping up the game of being the fabulous Flynn.

LAST DAYS

Errol phoned me to say that he was taking off for the West Coast. Why he was headed back to California he didn't say, but while he was in Los Angeles he agreed to do three days of filming for a TV show. Part way through it he quit: he was finished, weary, couldn't feel what he was doing. "Sorry," he said to the producer, "I just can't finish it."

I heard that he stayed around the porch of a hotel in Los Angeles rereading the galleys of *Wicked Ways*. Writers often get a kick out of seeing books in the galley stage.

Maybe he figured the book was his last big show.

I'm sure he did.

He liked what he read and told me so.

The house was finished in Jamaica and he needed to pay the builders: that or his general expenses were still heavy.

There was a prospective buyer for his beloved *Zaca*. Up in Vancouver. Sell the *Zaca*.

He took Dhondi along to Canada.

• • •

211

And now—could it be?—as an actor he knew when to take a final bow, when to leave the stage, when and what kind of a curtain might look just right.

I have the feeling that when he went to Vancouver, intending to sell the *Zaca* for $100,000—I have the feeling he knew that the greatest way to announce his book was not to come back out front of the curtain for another bow.

To die just before the book came out.

What a performance!

Am I imagining that just because it happened that way?

He had a flair for the dramatic: had that from infancy on, and it was bigger and better than ever in him now.

There were the headlines: October 14, 1959—Errol Flynn Dead at Vancouver.

The dynamo was laid to rest.

I heard strange stories after his death.

I heard that his body was four days going south to Los Angeles on a freight train, with somebody sitting on the rough box all the way.

Four days on a freight train going south. On the bum for the last time. Down through Washington State, down through Oregon, down through California.

Jim Laxton, the stunt man, sitting in for Errol. Sitting on him: sitting on the rough box that carried the New Guinea roustabout to Forest Lawn in Los Angeles.

Somebody took a photo of the box as it left Vancouver. Somebody else was at the other end to photograph the return of the swashbuckler.

Talk about the lonesome road.

I was told that he had been entertaining a group of people in Vancouver, talking to them, recounting stories of his life, and that during this time a drug was working upon him, that he then asked to be excused while he went to sleep for a while.

The medical report said it was a massive heart attack.

In the carousels of the world's playlands there is a brass ring you reach for as the merry-go-round turns. The children of the world (of whatever age) reach eagerly for the ring, and if they catch it they get—what? Another ride, a free ride.

Now and then one of the grapplers for a brass ring wakes up to discover that the thing he has reached for is indeed exactly that—nothing more than a ring, a bit of copper and zinc, casual metals of the earth.

Maybe it wasn't the ring they were after but the ride, the reaching out, the action, the sensation, winning or missing, the expression of the energy.

Errol woke late to discover he was reaching for a dubious alloy of copper and zinc and began to doubt the carousel, the ride, the reach, the prize.

When you question the nature of the brass ring you are done.

A HEADSTONE
FOR ERROL FLYNN

There were many mystifying acts in the last days of Errol Flynn.

Why did he undertake to build a large house on a Jamaican promontory overlooking the ocean when at the same time he was so busy snooking about for an end of it all? Did he have in mind a mausoleum to be known one day as Errol Flynn House? If not, why did he point to a spot behind the house and tell me that there was where he wanted to be interred?

And consider the anomaly, that at Forest Lawn Cemetery in Los Angeles where he was buried on October 20, 1959, and where Jack Warner read the eulogy, no gravestone marks his grave seventeen years after his burial.

Why not? Was there no money in the estate, no interest in that detail in his family, among his three wives, by Hollywood as an industry? Among his fans?

Does it mean nobody loved him or cared about him but that many were willing to use him or bask in his aura?

Is it possible that in the two-million-dollar estate he left

214

there wasn't five hundred bucks for a marker half a foot high to read:

ERROL FLYNN
Born Hobart, Tasmania, June 20, 1909
Died October 14, 1959

As this is written, no such gravestone exists.

There is the big house along the North Shore of Jamaica, and there is his spirit.

The rest is at Forest Lawn.

He was divided by life, and so he is in death.

What interested me primarily in Errol was that I beheld in him the peculiar parameter in man: the creative height that resides in humans alongside the base instinct; his high creative impulse and his actual wicked capacity for predatoriness in some situations and with some people. There it was, in him, like a gyroscope that turned and spiraled upward, and in the same gyration it could turn back down. And he went about life this way from minute to minute all day, all year, all life.

His physical beauty may have been his undoing.

When he was young nobody referred to him as handsome. He was always described as beautiful, an appellation usually reserved for attractive women. He was rarely called handsome, only that other hallowed term.

It gave him a propulsion, a problem, a confidence. And it was also his Achilles heel.

The first victim of his beauty was his literary aspiration, his desire to become a writer.

His physical attraction cast him as an actor, where all

could see that rare form, that wonderful face, his perfection of feature and the animal magnetism that went with all the rest. It was his strength and his weakness, his doing and undoing.

I think he would have enjoyed this account of himself, this "study." Anything except total silence. Much as he seemed to crave and look for peace, he also wanted the noise of the world about him. And after he rested he always went seeking it—in wars, in sea voyages, in the female heart.

Errol Flynn will remain something far beyond and more complex than a mere Casanova of the world's boudoirs. He deserves a far larger context than that, not limited by his travels over the seas, by his more than fifty films, by his descendants, by the famed book he lived, but only by the breadth of his mammalian contradiction, the mystery of his animal scope. Within him something of each and all of us resides—angel and devil, war and peace, hope and dread.

I have often heard people remark, speaking of some famed person who has gotten into trouble or wound up badly (the fate of many such figures), "Don't waste your pity on So-and-so." The comment that follows is something like this: he or she had money, fame, a great life.

With Errol, too, I don't think pity is the issue or the answer or an explanation. Whether rich or poor, famous or anonymous, creative or nascent, man's fate is all too often a sad one, pitiful while great, wonderful while inexplicable, a quest without ending or answers.

Errol can't be dismissed—at least I don't dismiss him—as merely an actor, a Casanova, a wandering Odyssean character.

While working on his autobiography I was searching for a word to summarize him and it escaped me. Sometimes it seemed to half surface and then subside. But one day the word arrived. It came when the sun was scorching, the water Errol submerged himself in was the deep Atlantic, the breathable air was sultry and provocative, and the earth beneath our feet seemed especially volcanic and alive. Fire, water, air and earth. Errol was elemental, that was it. Elemental was Errol. He fitted Jamaica and Jamaica fitted him. Maybe he fitted the world and the world fitted him, in somewhat the same way. I realized I had never before beheld and been so close to a human who was such incessant fire and water, air and earth.

My view is that part of the explanation of Errol Flynn has to be in biological terms. It was not exclusively a feud between himself and his mother, though that was a factor too; not the divagations and turns and spirals into which his ambition took him, though this was part of what happened to him; and not other explanations that fall into the domain of psychiatrist, sociologist or any of the other usual -ists or -isms.

He was a specialty of nature: a biological entity unique to himself.

Some persons are born very tall or very short, will grow very fat or stay terribly lean, will have a character of lifetime listlessness or restlessness. Some people are born with a genetic character, some inner mechanism that says they can, if careful, live to a hundred; others with a defect that says they will be dead by the age of three. In the same way Errol Flynn had gigantic energy: he had the energy of two or three people, not just one. His energy and the expenditure thereof led him into both accomplishment and waste.

Few men, including professional deep-sea divers, spent

more time under water than he. Others would have been trapped and died in waters fifty and a hundred feet below many times, when this man powerfully swam to the surface and saved his life—and enjoyed the thrill.

His drinking would have killed most men ten years earlier than he was affected by it. The same is true for his drug intake: he absorbed far more than many or most other beings could safely take.

What kind of being was this? How do you explain him? "My job is to defy the normal." He said this over and over, and he did it.

He had an excess of physical energy, and his life and what he did with it was in large part a result of the ways he expended this excess.

For some time I wondered who Errol reminded me of in fiction or legend. He had a tall, erect carriage, he flailed his sword cane occasionally, and he had his own gallant objectives—mainly females. Then it occurred to me: he was a fourth cousin of Don Quixote, but that far removed from the Don.

Errol threw his body at the world trying to extract sensations out of it, as Quixote flailed his sword against injustices real and imagined, at windmills, at whole gangs of enemies at one time. And precisely as Don Quixote came away from his duels beaten in body, defeated in his objectives, so I beheld Errol having a similar experience, drawing a similar non sequitur for his efforts.

His participation in the Spanish Civil War and the Castro uprising were distinctly Quixote adventures: and he went about them left-handedly in the amusing, droll, poignancy and alarum that characterized the adventures of his Spanish spiritual ancestor. After that Errol was totally original; he must attack the sources of sensation in the world—females, drugs, alcohol, foods—and bend them to his will, extract from them the quintessence of their essences, the pleasure dome achieve. He must taste life to the full, even the dregs, to achieve the highest possible human orgasm: this was the justice in his soul.

Alas, after his morphine, he could have vile painful withdrawal symptoms: his nerves screeching, another bout lost. After his vodka he woke in chatters that stayed about him for hours, and his liver withered away: another defeat. With females, sheer conquest—until one or the other took him for a million bucks, or an estate, or drained his essential nature to boredom. Always he was knocked flat: his famous tiger-headed sword cane lying beside him, figuratively at least till he rose and recuperated and then did battle again with the sources of pleasure, sensation, physical gratification.

He would slay the God of Hedonism.

Alas, the great god laid him low at last at the age of fifty —about twenty-five years before he might have been destined, with other lesser pursuits of the flesh, to expire.

In dealing with Errol Flynn we are dealing with fable. "Fabulous" is the most casually used word in the American media, yet it usually refers to matters not fabled at all, and in the same casual vernacular as "colossal" and "magnificent."

With Errol we are in the realm of the truly fabled: he is the physical being, the world-rover, the master of the seas, the living Ulysses. But there was another dimension of his existence which is unknown. What he wanted to be, what he hoped, what he worked for, his dream: this was part of the fable that was never realized.

Still he was of the proportion of those heroes who have shadowed the world, leaving us a book, a statue, a legend, a tale, some unbelievable thing: adding to the concept of The Fable that is Man, helping explain us to ourselves.

APPENDIX

THE MOTION PICTURES

In the Wake of the Bounty, 1933
Murder at Monte Carlo, 1935
The Case of the Curious Bride, 1935
Don't Bet on Blondes, 1935
Captain Blood, 1935
The Charge of the Light Brigade, 1936
Green Light, 1937
The Prince and the Pauper, 1937
Another Dawn, 1937
The Perfect Specimen, 1937
The Adventures of Robin Hood, 1938
Four's a Crowd, 1938
The Sisters, 1938
Dawn Patrol, 1938
Dodge City, 1939
The Private Lives of Elizabeth and Essex, 1939
Virginia City, 1940
The Sea Hawk, 1940
Santa Fe Trail, 1940
Footsteps in the Dark, 1941

Dive Bomber, 1941
They Died with Their Boots On, 1941
Desperate Journey, 1942
Gentleman Jim, 1942
Edge of Darkness, 1943
Thank Your Lucky Stars, 1943
Northern Pursuit, 1943
Uncertain Glory, 1944
Objective Burma, 1945
San Antonio, 1945
Never Say Goodbye, 1946
Cry Wolf, 1947
Escape Me Never, 1947
Silver River, 1948
Adventures of Don Juan, 1948
It's a Great Feeling, 1948
That Forsyte Woman, 1949
Montana, 1950
Rocky Mountain 1950
Kim, 1950
Hello, God, 1950
Adventures of Captain Fabian, 1951
Mara Maru, 1952
Against All Flags, 1952
The Master of Ballantrae, 1953
Crossed Swords, 1954
Let's Make Up, 1955
The Warriors, 1955
King's Rhapsody, 1955
Istanbul, 1957
The Big Boodle, 1957
The Sun Also Rises, 1957
Too Much, Too Soon, 1958
The Roots of Heaven, 1958
Cuban Rebel Girls, 1959